CONTENTS

ABOUT THE AUTHOR

Alan Vincent graduated with a French degree from Reading University. After teaching in Nigeria and Hertfordshire, he became Head of Guidance and Admissions for the North Oxfordshire Centre of Advanced Studies. Since 1994 he has worked as the Coordinator for the North Oxfordshire Learning Partnership and Manager of the local Education Business Partnership. He is also a SETPoint, responsible for coordinating information based on Science, Technology, Engineering and Mathematics for the area of Oxfordshire, Buckinghamshire and Milton Keynes.

Alan was President of the National Association of Careers and Guidance Teachers (NACGT) from 1985 to 1987 and is currently the General Secretary. Throughout his career he has made significant contributions to the development of careers education and guidance, for example through his involvement in training courses run by NACGT, ICG, CRAC, LEAs and TECs.

How to Choose Your GCSEs

Essential Information about Key Stage 4
Courses and Examinations

SEVENTH EDITION

Alan Vincent

TROTMAN

This seventh edition published in 2001 in Great Britain by
Trotman & Company Ltd, 2 The Green, Richmond, Surrey TW9 1PL

© Trotman and Company Limited

British Library Cataloguing in Publication Data
A catalogue record for this book is available from the British Library

ISBN 0 85660 668 5

Typeset by Mac Style, Scarborough, N. Yorkshire
Printed and bound in Great Britain by Creative Print & Design (Wales) Ltd

GLOSSARY OF ABBREVIATIONS

ACCAC	Qualifications, Curriculum & Assessment Authority for Wales
AEB	Associated Examining Board
A-level	Advanced Level
AQA	Assessment and Qualifications Alliance
AS level	Advanced Subsidiary (formerly Advanced Supplementary) Level
BA	Bachelor of Arts degree
BEd	Bachelor of Education degree
BTEC	Business & Technology Education Council (now part of Edexcel Foundation)
CCEA	Council for the Curriculum, Examinations & Assessment (Northern Ireland)
CLCI	Careers Library Classification Index
COIC	Careers and Occupational Information Centre
CRAC	Careers Research & Advisory Centre
CSYS	Certificate of Sixth Year Studies (in Scotland)
DENI	Department for Education for Northern Ireland
DfEE	Department for Education & Employment
EAB	Examinations Appeals Board
ECCTIS	Educational Counselling and Credit Transfer Information Service
GCSE	General Certificate of Secondary Education
GNVQ	General National Vocational Qualification
GOML	Graded Objective in Modern Languages
GRC	Grade Related Criteria (Scotland)
H Grade	Higher Grade (Scotland)
HMI	Her Majesty's Inspectorate
HNC	Higher National Certificate
HND	Higher National Diploma
ICG	Institute of Career Guidance
ICT	Information & Communications Technology
IGCSE	International GCSE
KS	Key Stage
LEA	Local Education Authority
MEG	Midland Examining Group
NACGT	National Association of Careers & Guidance Teachers

NEAB	Northern Examinations & Assessment Board
NNEB	National Nursery Examination Board
NVQ	National Vocational Qualification
OCR	Oxford, Cambridge and RSA Examinations
OFSTED	Office for Standards in Education
QCA	Qualifications & Curriculum Authority
RSA	Royal Society for Arts
S Grade	Standard Grade (Scotland)
SCE	Scottish Certificate of Education
SEG	Southern Examining Group
SGA	Scottish Group Award
SQA	Scottish Qualifications Authority
SVQ	Scottish Vocational Qualification
TEC	Training & Enterprise Council
UCAS	Universities & Colleges Admissions Service
WJEC	Welsh Joint Education Committee

1. GETTING THE FACTS STRAIGHT

The GCSE countdown for you has now begun. What are you letting your-self in for? Let's begin by getting a few of the facts straight.

What is the GCSE?

GCSE stands for the General Certificate of Secondary Education.

Who is the GCSE for?

YOU. It is designed as a two-year course of study for students in Years 10 and 11 (Years 11 and 12 in Northern Ireland).

At Key Stage 4 (KS4) GCSE is the main means of assessing attainment. The criteria for GCSE examinations are in line with the National Curriculum for KS4.

Can everybody take the GCSE?

Yes. The GCSE is open to anyone who can meet its requirements, regardless of their age or circumstances of study. The GCSE is therefore available to both mature and private candidates as well as all those in schools and colleges.

In 2000 over five and a half million GCSE entries, or about 22 million papers, were marked by the awarding bodies.

When do I take the exam?

The usual age to sit the end-of-course exam is 16 . . . but there are no hard and fast rules. You can take it before or after that age.

There is some more information about taking the GCSE early and its implications in the next chapter – GCSE and the National Curriculum.

When can I sit the exam?

There are two sittings each year. Most students will take the exam in the summer when all subjects are on offer. In most subjects the exams are held in the period from mid-May to the end of June. The awarding bodies organise a common timetable, one that sees their different written examinations for the main subjects taking place at the same time.

Oral tests for Modern Foreign Languages and English speaking and listening tests are usually taken earlier, with dates set by schools, within a timescale laid down by the awarding bodies.

There are some changes to the normal schedule from summer 2001. GCSE written papers in English Literature and Geography are to be moved back from May to June, in order to give teachers more time to prepare students. Some papers in subjects with fewer entries are to be brought forward from June to May.

The second sitting is in either November or January, depending on what course you are taking. Not all subjects are offered in these autumn or winter examinations.

What are the awarding bodies?

These are the organisations that design the syllabuses for GCSE examinations, within criteria set by the national qualifications authorities. For England and Wales, there are now only four awarding bodies.

AQA (Northern Office)
Devas Street
Manchester M15 6EX
0161 953 1180
http://www.neab.ac.uk

AQA (Southern Office)
Stag Hill House
Guildford
Surrey GU2 5XJ
01483 506506
http://www.aeb.org.uk

EDEXCEL Foundation
Stewart House
32 Russell Square
London WC1B 5DP
020 7393 4444
http://www.edexcel.org.uk

OCR
Syndicate Buildings
1 Hills Road
Cambridge CB1 2EU
01223 553311
http://www.ocr.org.uk

Welsh Joint Education Committee
245 Western Avenue
Cardiff CF5 2YX
029 2026 5000
http://www.wjec.co.uk

Most schools select more than one awarding body. Teachers can then choose the GCSE syllabus that they think best meets their students' needs. Remember, though, that all the syllabuses are based on the same National Curriculum programmes of study.

Why do I need to take the GCSE?

Sixteen is a turning point in every young person's life. It's a time of change. Some of you may leave school and take a job or start on a training placement. Most of you will stay on in full-time education, at either school or college, for at least one or two more years, in order to improve your range of skills and qualifications. For some the aim will be to take further examinations, such as AS/A-levels or a General National Vocational Qualification (GNVQ), and perhaps go on to university or a college of higher education.

For everyone, GCSE offers an opportunity to assess your skills and abilities and help you decide how you can improve these and use them to direct you along more specific lines.

What makes the GCSE different from examinations in the past?

GCSE is designed to relate to students' everyday lives. For example, syllabuses address economic, political, social and environmental matters, where these are appropriate and relevant to the particular subject. They also provide opportunities for the appropriate use of Information & Communications Technology (ICT), to complement and support work done in that particular subject.

With the GCSE there is more emphasis on problem solving and using the knowledge you have gained. That is why GCSE courses include practical work, oral work, fieldwork, investigations, projects and even group work. As a result, courses are more interesting, more inventive and more useful. It all means less time being a passive learner and more time spent on projects, problem solving and finding out for yourself.

From 2002, the government plans to introduce Vocational GCSEs – offered in subjects which will be even more closely related to job options.

For more information on Vocational GCSEs and other vocational alternatives, see Chapter 7 – The Vocational Alternative.

Most GCSEs include coursework – that's work that you do during the two years. And the marks for your coursework count towards your final result. Exams are fine for testing knowledge and, to some extent, understanding. But they favour people with a good memory and there are many skills that an exam can't test at all. How, for example, can an exam show how good you are at looking up information and using it? Or at carrying out your own project? The GCSE format will not only test your knowledge of formulae for scientific experiments, but also how well you apply them in the lab. After all, what use is it being able to remember something you don't understand and are not able to use?

This is where the GCSE scores – it is designed to test ALL your skills.

2. GCSE AND THE NATIONAL CURRICULUM

What is the National Curriculum?

The Education Reform Act of 1988 requires all maintained schools to provide a broad and balanced curriculum for students of compulsory school age. This is known as the National Curriculum.

What subjects are included in the National Curriculum?

At present, the National Curriculum consists of eleven subjects – with Welsh as an additional subject for Welsh-speaking schools.

In Key Stages 1–3 the following subjects are included in the National Curriculum:

- English
- Mathematics
- Science
- Design & Technology
- Information & Communications Technology
- History
- Geography
- Art & Design
- Music
- Physical Education
- and a Modern Foreign Language

At Key Stage 4 the range of subjects that students may study and in which they may be tested is increased, but the only subjects with compulsory programmes of study are:

- English
- Mathematics
- Science
- Design & Technology
- ICT
- a Modern Foreign Language
- Physical Education
- Citizenship (compulsory from Autumn 2002)

In Wales Welsh is added for schools that are not Welsh speaking. Wales also has separate subject Orders from England in History, Geography, Art, Music and Welsh.

Schools in England and Wales also have to provide identified Religious Education, Careers Education and Sex Education. With Sex Education, as with Religious Education, parents (or guardians) can choose *not* to let their child study the subject (except for the elements of Sex Education required by the National Curriculum ie human growth and reproduction).

What effect does the National Curriculum have on GCSE?

There are National Curriculum guidelines on the knowledge, skills and understanding that all students are expected to have acquired in each subject by the ages of 7 (age 8 in Northern Ireland), 11, 14 and 16.

GCSE is the main means of assessing what students have achieved in each subject during KS4. GNVQ also makes a significant contribution for a large number of young people – either through the experience of specific units or through the Part One GNVQ qualification. There is further information on the role of GNVQ in KS4 in Chapter 7.

GCSE criteria have been revised over the past few years, in line with changes to the National Curriculum itself. New syllabuses take account of the knowledge, understanding and skills young students ought to be acquiring. Progression and continuity receive greater emphasis, with, for example, the need to ensure the appropriate links between KS3 and KS4.

The following subjects are due for further changes to their GCSE specification from 2001, with an effect on examinations in 2003:

- English
- Mathematics
- Science (single and double award)

In these and the other National Curriculum subjects, all syllabuses cover the KS4 programmes of study. These programmes of study define the essential content of each subject and are the basis for planning, teaching, learning and assessment objectives.

There are also a number of approved syllabuses in subjects that do not have subject-specific criteria. These syllabuses are governed by the GCSE Regulations alone.

Will this make a difference to me? Will I have any choice about taking the National Curriculum subjects?

The National Curriculum takes some of the optional element out of the 14–16 stage.

Most students will take GCSEs in English, Mathematics and Science. For Science, you may take:

- a double award exam (equal to two GCSEs) that covers Biology, Chemistry and Physics;
- separate exams in these three science subjects; or
- a single award exam (equal to one GCSE) that covers all three science subjects, but less fully than the double award.

The Science option that you are offered may depend to some extent on your school's curriculum policies. But the government believes that most students should take Double Science or the three separate sciences. The alternative Single Science course is intended only for a minority of students who need to spend more time on other subjects.

One important point is that the student who takes Single Science but who then wishes to take AS/A-level Science post-16 may need a bridging course before (or at the start of) the AS/A-levels.

The National Curriculum is not intended to be a straitjacket and there is an increasing amount of flexibility. In some circumstances, a school may decide that a pupil will achieve better results at KS4 without having to take all the normally compulsory National Curriculum subjects. This is referred to as *disapplication* of the National Curriculum.

What does 'disapplication' mean?

At KS4 the school can disapply a student from either *one* or *two* of the following subjects – Science, Design & Technology and a Modern Foreign Language. There has to be a clear reason for disapplication. It can only happen if it allows a student to take part in one of the following:

1. a substantial work-related learning programme (eg a work placement with a training element, or a college course for one or two days a week);
2. additional studies in a subject area where the student has a particular strength (eg taking a second foreign language);
3. a programme to help learning across the curriculum (eg a literacy or numeracy programme).

Science can only be disapplied for the first of the above reasons.

Essentially it is up to schools to suggest disapplication, but they should then consult with you and your parents (or guardians). And you have the right to make the final decision – you can carry on with the National Curriculum subject if you want to.

Formal disapplication may not be necessary for students to do some of the things mentioned above. There may be sufficient flexibility in the school's curriculum and timetable to allow you to fulfil the full National Curriculum but also take on extended work experience, for example.

In Wales there is even more time for schools to use as they choose because there are no requirements for Modern Foreign Languages, Technology or ICT.

What about short courses as an alternative?

Short courses, as an alternative to a full GCSE, are available in:

- Art & Design
- Design & Technology
- Geography
- History
- ICT
- Modern Foreign Languages
- Music
- Physical Education
- Religious Education
- Welsh Second Language
- Business Studies (from September 2001)
- Electronics (from September 2001)

Some of these options, particularly Religious Education, are proving very popular. The courses are set at the same standard as the 'full' GCSEs but have half the value. They take up half the teaching time – so they might, for example, be completed in one year rather than the usual two. Short courses are graded on the same scale as the full GCSE, but cover fewer topics.

Short course exams often use the same questions and exam papers as full GCSEs. The same A* to G grades are used, and short courses are recorded as half a GCSE in the performance or 'league' tables.

You can use the short courses in different ways:

- More able students can use them as a way of taking more subjects, eg fitting in a second foreign language that might not otherwise be possible.
- If other subject choices prevent you from taking a full GCSE you can still gain a short course qualification in a subject.
- If you think that you may need extra time to study a particular subject, taking a short course GCSE in the time taken by a full GCSE course may be an attractive idea.

Remember that you will be allowed to drop one or more subjects at the end of KS3, if this seems a good option for you.

Also, you will be able, either individually or on a whole class basis, to take GCSE early and then to drop the subjects that have been taken.

More information about alternatives to GCSE is included at the end of this chapter.

What will be the effects of my taking one or more GCSEs early?

There are specific National Curriculum Regulations that apply to whole classes of students taking GCSE (or equivalent) qualifications early. Students who take GCSE (or an equivalent qualification) in a National Curriculum subject at the same time as the majority of students in their class, and before the start of the second year of KS4, will from that time be exempt from the National Curriculum requirements relating to that subject. This exemption applies whatever the level attained by the student in the examination. However, it does *not* apply to a short course, when both a full course and a short course are specified for the particular National Curriculum subject.

The government has encouraged schools to enter students for one or more subjects early if they are ready. It wants the number of bright students taking early GCSEs to increase, to encourage higher expectations. In practice, record numbers of students *are* taking GCSE early. Nearly 45,000 took at least one GCSE before they turned 15 in 1999. In 1996 only 30,600 took GCSEs before they were 15.

In 2000 two six-year-old children broke the existing record by passing GCSE ICT. A special government scheme was due to see 500 nine- and ten-year-olds sitting GCSE in 2001.

The Secretary of State for Education thinks that eventually 5% of candidates could be taking the exam by the age of 14.

What are the alternatives to GCSE?

At KS4, as at post-16 level, the GNVQ has become a popular alternative.

GNVQ courses are offered at Foundation, Intermediate and Advanced levels and teach work-related knowledge, skills and understanding. Students are expected to acquire the basic skills and knowledge relevant to a particular vocational area, such as Art & Design, Business, Health & Social Care, Leisure & Tourism (Leisure & Recreation at Advanced level), or Manufacturing.

At present, GNVQ at KS4 can mean any of the following:

- a Part One GNVQ at Foundation or Intermediate level
- a full, six-unit GNVQ at Foundation or Intermediate level

- GNVQ units
- units of a vocational A-level (formerly Advanced GNVQ).

Vocational GCSEs are soon to replace Foundation, Intermediate and Part One GNVQs. They will be introduced in September 2002 and will be based on the Part One GNVQ, so they will be equivalent to at least two GCSEs (and possibly as many as four).

For more general information about GNVQs at Key Stage 4 and vocational GCSEs see Chapter 7 – The Vocational Alternative. Additional information about GNVQs post-16 is contained in Chapter 13 – Life After GCSE.

What about key skills?

Young people should be developing a range of 'Key Skills' that will be helpful to them in adult, working life. The National Curriculum is the main vehicle for the development of the Key Skills. A new Key Skills qualification consisting of Communication, Application of Number and Information Technology is now included as an approved qualification for Key Stage 4. You should be able to find out from your school if this qualification is offered. Chapter 7 also contains important information about Key Skills in the context of the vocational options.

Is there anything else?

Yes. From September 2000 more able 14–16-year-olds can bypass some subjects at GCSE, by taking an Advanced Subsidiary (AS) course in Modern Languages and/or Design & Technology. Taking AS at 16 would allow these gifted students to take A-level a year earlier, at age 17. It is also possible for the most able young people to drop a Modern Foreign Language or Design & Technology to concentrate on particular subjects.

While GNVQs are about work, they do not offer training for a particular job. This is more the role of NVQs (National Vocational Qualifications). These are normally available for people who have left school and are already at work or in training placements. At KS4 some students may work towards an NVQ or NVQ units, if they are on a regular or 'extended' work experience placement, following a course at a further education college and/or working with a training provider. There is more information about NVQs in Chapter 7 – The Vocational Alternative.

There are also increasing opportunities for students who are unlikely to achieve GCSE grade G, Foundation GNVQ or NVQ level 1. 'Entry level' awards are available in a range of National Curriculum subjects and in vocational areas such as retail, leisure and tourism and manufacturing.

These non-GCSE awards have to be approved by QCA (or by ACCAC in Wales or the CCEA in Northern Ireland). Entry level awards in basic skills, such as literacy and numeracy, are also available.

Less able or underachieving students can now use disapplication time to concentrate on practical skills, eg taking vocational language courses as an alternative to GCSE, or a practical science course that is equivalent to four GCSEs.

There are a few other qualifications that your school might be offering at KS4, below the level of GCSE or GNVQ. Such qualifications have to feature on an approved list published by the DfEE and QCA. They include:

- certain qualifications in Literacy, Numeracy and Information Technology that are meant to offer progression towards GCSE or the Key Skills units;
- some qualifications in other National Curriculum subjects.

Some students will not be entered for GCSE in a National Curriculum subject nor for a designated qualification relating to that subject below GCSE. For such students teacher assessment of performance at the end of KS4 will be recorded, normally via the National Record of Achievement.

To recap, the main courses at KS4 are as follows:

- full GCSEs
- GCSE short courses
- vocational GCSEs (from Autumn 2002)
- Part One GNVQs
- full GNVQs in approved subjects
- individual units from approved GNVQ subjects
- NVQs or NVQ units
- Entry Level Certificates.

Where Welsh is a core subject students will take Welsh to GCSE. In schools where Welsh is a non-core foundation subject students will study Welsh at KS4, but not necessarily to GCSE. A short course is available in Welsh as a second language. GNVQ Welsh Language units are also available for KS4 students studying Welsh as a second language.

There is also an International GCSE (IGCSE), but this is mainly for overseas students.

Important addresses in England and Wales

Department for Education and Employment
Sanctuary Buildings

Great Smith Street
Westminster
London SW1P 3BT
020 7925 5000
Website: www.dfee.gov.uk

The Qualifications and Curriculum Authority
83 Piccadilly
London W1J 8QA
020 7509 5555
Website: www.qca.org.uk

Welsh National Assembly, Training and Education Department
Cathays Park
Cardiff CF1 3NQ
Tel: 029 2082 5111
Website: www.wales.gov.uk

3. HOW THE GCSE EXAM WORKS

Following recent mergers there are now just five awarding bodies that set examinations for GCSE and GNVQs at KS4:

* *Assessment and Qualifications Alliance (AQA)* bringing together the Associated Examining Board (AEB), Northern Examinations and Assessment Board (NEAB), Southern Examining Group (SEG) and City & Guilds.
* *EDEXCEL Foundation*
* *OCR* bringing together Oxford & Cambridge, The Midland Examining Group (MEG) and RSA Examinations Board.
* *The Welsh Joint Education Committee (WJEC)*
* *The Northern Ireland Council for the Curriculum, Examinations and Assessment (CCEA).*

Your school will normally be free to select courses of study set by any of the awarding bodies. Most teachers look carefully at the full range of syllabuses to find the course that seems the most interesting and useful – the one they hope you will enjoy and do best in.

With different groups setting the exams in the same subjects, do standards vary?

In the past government statements and reports from HMI have raised concern about the consistency of standards. In particular, the awarding bodies were asked to apply more objective criteria and to be more rigorous in their approaches and procedures.

GCSE general criteria from QCA provide overall guidance on subject titles, the nature of syllabuses, assessment procedures and the general conduct of examinations. These general criteria require each syllabus to promote a balance of knowledge, understanding and skills. They also demand that student achievement in each syllabus is assessed through a combination of coursework and terminal examination appropriate to the subject.

In England, Wales and Northern Ireland the awarding bodies together form the Joint Council for General Qualifications. The Joint Council provides a forum for discussion and the exchange of information. It is responsible for coordinating the work of the individual bodies and helping to establish nationally consistent practices. The awarding bodies, for example, collaborated over the preparation of GCSE syllabuses for the

National Curriculum core subjects of English, Mathematics and Science. Each group put forward proposals to the Joint Council. From these proposals a range of syllabuses was agreed by the Joint Council for General Qualifications. As a consequence, for each core subject there are now syllabuses catering for the full range of needs.

All these moves ensure that syllabuses have the highest possible degree of consistency. QCA works closely with the Joint Council and the individual awarding bodies to maintain GCSE standards and to continue to improve the effectiveness and fairness of the system.

How is the GCSE graded?

The grading system is based on an A*–G scale. The top grade, a 'starred' A grade (A*) has been available since 1994.

Examiners decide the grade boundaries for the award of grades A, C and F. The remaining grades are then awarded on an arithmetical basis. For example, for a particular syllabus the grade A boundary might be set at 300 marks and the grade C boundary at 220 marks. The grade B boundary would then be set halfway, at 260 marks.

In Modern Foreign Languages there is a separate awarding system. A range of points – usually 7 – is available for each of the four language skills. GCSE grades are awarded on the number of points achieved in the subject as a whole. So, for example, an A grade is awarded for candidates who achieve 24 or more of the 28 points usually available.

In order to help parents understand the level of attainment signified by the GCSE grade awarded, 'attainment descriptions' are offered that relate to grades A, C and F and below G.

How difficult is it to achieve the A*?

There is no limit on the number of starred A grades awarded in any one subject. Results depend on the quality of the candidate's work and on where the awarding body draws its other grade boundaries.

What happens if my GCSE performance does not earn a grade G or above?

If that does happen, the performance is reported on the results slip as U (for 'unclassified').

How will the marks for my GCSE be decided?

In most subjects, the marks are made up of two parts.

Firstly, coursework done in Years 10 and 11 (Years 11 and 12 in Northern

Ireland) is assessed. Secondly, an examination is held at the end of the two years. This is explained more fully in the next chapter.

Will I lose marks for bad spelling?

QCA has developed marking criteria for use in GCSE terminal examinations. They apply to all subjects where candidates are required to write in sentences (in English or Welsh). They apply to all GCSE written papers *and* written coursework, but not to multiple choice or practical tests.

For each GCSE subject 5–10% of the marks for each written paper can be deducted for errors in spelling, punctuation and grammar.

The assessment criteria for English and Welsh make additional requirements for linguistic accuracy. Performance in spelling, punctuation and grammar are factors in determining the candidate's overall grade.

Does this mean that dictionaries cannot be used in examinations?

Dictionaries and spelling aids are not normally allowed, except for certain vocational examinations and for candidates who are permitted to use a bilingual dictionary (after the school has made a special representation and the awarding body has agreed).

Following the latest National Curriculum changes the use of dictionaries in modern foreign languages exams is now banned. Candidates will be allowed to use dictionaries for internally assessed coursework, but not in externally assessed exams.

Are there any special arrangements for those with a disability?

Yes. The awarding bodies have special arrangements to ensure that those with a permanent or long-term disability are not disadvantaged in assessment. Special arrangements can only be made following an application from the headteacher or principal and this must be accompanied by medical or other appropriate evidence (eg an educational psychologist's report).

One fairly common concession is to allow up to 25% extra time for written examinations, allowing candidates who have particular difficulties with reading or writing more time to read the paper and to plan and correct their answers.

This has sometimes been a contentious area, with some inconsistency in awarding body practice. It is well worth parents and/or guardians thoroughly exploring the situation with school staff at an early stage, if there is any possibility of such arrangements being applicable.

There is also further information in the DfEE leaflet 'Special educational needs – a guide for parents' (available free by phoning 08000 96 66 26).

Do employers understand what GCSEs are?

Every attempt has been made to let employers know about recent changes. But you might still find yourself faced with a bewildered employer or personnel officer. Don't worry . . . help is available. On the back of the examination certificate you will receive there is an explanation of how the exam works.

4. COURSEWORK IN FOCUS

We've mentioned 'coursework' several times. Now it's time to look at it in more detail.

What is coursework?

Coursework is work which is integral to the course, meaning that much of it is done in class and is closely supervised by teachers.

It can take various forms such as assignments in English, History, Religious Studies; field work in Geography; practical and project work in Art, Mathematics, Technology and Science; compositions in Music.

Throughout your two years of study for GCSEs your teacher will set specific topics for you to do. These topics will be marked by your teacher and the marks will go towards your final GCSE results.

Why is coursework necessary?

As mentioned previously, many skills can't be tested by the traditional written exam – practical and oral skills, for example. Coursework gives you the chance to demonstrate the many abilities you have and so makes the final mark you receive much fairer.

Teachers, with support from the awarding bodies, are responsible for ensuring that students take on suitable coursework. HMI and OFSTED reports on quality and standards in GCSE examinations have found that both teacher assessment and the guidance provided by the awarding bodies to support teacher assessment of coursework are generally of a high standard.

Which skills and abilities are tested through coursework?

Your performance in coursework will show if you are able to:

- research, collect, compare and organise information
- work in a group
- make accurate records and use your powers of observation through laboratory and field work
- plan and organise a long piece of work
- use apparatus and machinery

- communicate – and that means to listen as well as to talk and discuss
- investigate, plan and design.

These are exactly the work skills that employers value.

Coursework also encourages students to work independently and helps them prepare for higher level studies, such as AS/A-levels.

When will I do the coursework?

In some subjects you will start coursework during the first term of Year 10 (Year 11 in Northern Ireland), while with other subjects coursework may not start until Year 11 (Year 12 in Northern Ireland). It will all depend on the syllabus.

Yes, but when will I actually do coursework? Will it cut into my spare time?

Some of the work will be done in class, some will be done as homework. Though your teachers may say it shouldn't take you any longer than your normal homework, it's only fair to say it probably will take more time, if you want to do well.

Is there coursework in all subjects?

Most Modern Foreign Languages include an oral, but there isn't necessarily any other coursework.

What percentage of marks is given for coursework?

There must always be an externally set terminal examination. In the case of modular syllabuses the terminal examination must account for at least 50% of the marks.

The weighting for coursework in all other syllabuses is set out below:

Art	up to 60%
Design & Technology	at least 40% and up to 60%
English	up to 40%
English Literature	up to 30%
Geography	at least 20% and up to 25%
History	up to 25%
Home Economics	up to 50%
ICT	at least 40% and up to 60%
Mathematics	up to 20%

Modern Foreign Languages	up to 30%
Music	up to 60%
Physical Education	at least 60% and up to 70%
Science	at least 25% and up to 30%
Welsh	at least 30% and up to 40%
Welsh Literature	up to 30%
Welsh Second Language	up to 40%

Do I have to worry about spelling in coursework?

When assessors are marking coursework, just as with exam papers, they will deduct marks for errors in the English – for poor spelling, punctuation or grammar. You could lose 5–10% of your potential marks.

It sounds as though I am going to have to take a lot of exams

It depends on how you look at it.

Your ability will be tested throughout the two years. But your coursework performance will in some cases enable you to go into the examination well on your way to a good grade.

What if six different teachers give me coursework at the same time – I'll be a wreck!

Coursework overload is a possible risk with the GCSE. Your teachers will be anxious to avoid overloading you. Nobody can tackle a great number of assignments at the same time and do them all well – and your teachers do want you to do well.

In a well-run school coursework overload should not happen. Before the two-year course begins teachers usually get together and work out a timetable for setting coursework assignments. But even the best-run systems can break down. So . . . if you are given too much coursework at any one time, don't keep your worries to yourself. Tell your teachers about the problem immediately.

No doubt you will find yourself working harder than before, but remember that your teachers are not trying to work you to a standstill. It is in their interests as well as yours that you do well.

Coursework is to your advantage

GCSE has been widely praised for allowing candidates to demonstrate what they know, understand and can do.

Coursework allows a wider range of skills to be assessed than is possible in a written examination. Evidence suggests that coursework assessment increases candidates' motivation:

- If you are a good communicator you'll have the chance to prove it.
- If you are a painstaking perfectionist you'll have the time to perfect your work and so earn marks for it.
- If you are a thinker you'll have time to think.
- If you are a problem solver you'll get the time to find the solution.

But . . . it's no good leaving everything to the last minute with GCSE. You won't get through by copying someone else's notes the day before the exam. You'll need to work throughout the two years to do well – and work hard. Sorry, but there's no escape.

What if I'm ill when an assessment is due?

You'll find that the deadlines set for coursework are quite flexible, so the odd week, even a month of illness, should not set you back too much.

But what if I'm away for a term or longer?

Most teachers and awarding bodies are very sympathetic if you are ill and will try to find a way for you to complete the course.

There are no hard and fast rules . . . subjects vary, and so do individual cases. But if you have completed enough pieces of coursework over the two years, they can usually assess how well you are likely to do, and give you a fair mark. However, one thing is certain. Both your school and awarding body want you to take the exam and will do their best to help you. So, if you know you are going to miss school for some reason, tell your teachers as soon as possible, so that they can make alternative arrangements for you.

What happens if I change schools in the middle of my GCSE?

In most cases it should not be too difficult for you to change from a course set by one awarding body to one set by another because they will both be assessing the same skills.

In addition, you might be able to transfer any coursework you have already completed. But – and it is a very big BUT – it depends on what subjects you are taking. The Joint Council for General Qualifications certainly recommends that assessment across syllabuses from more than one awarding body should be allowed.

For example, it is much easier to move from one syllabus to another in Maths or a Modern Foreign Language than it is, say, in History, where you could be studying a different historical period. And in English Literature the set books are unlikely to be the same so, again, transfer tends to be more difficult.

If you are well advanced in your original studies when you make the move then arrangements can be made for you to take the exam in your original course in your new school. Your teachers and the examiners will try and do their best for each student, so your case would be treated sympathetically.

My teacher doesn't like me. Will it affect my assessment marks?

No.

Equally, you can't be upgraded by your teacher either. You can rest assured there will be neither discrimination nor favouritism in your GCSE assessment. No teacher would allow any personal feelings to influence the results of a public examination. Besides which there are too many checks and safeguards . . . so it couldn't happen anyway. And all research shows that coursework is no less reliable than written examinations.

What's to stop someone doing my coursework for me?

The work you submit for assessment must be your own. Teachers have to certify that coursework has been supervised properly. And teachers are usually very shrewd: they know what most of their students are capable of.

If you quote from any books or other materials, you should state which sources you have used. And, if you receive guidance from someone other than your teacher, you should tell your teacher, who will then record the nature of the assistance.

Some teachers expect more of their students than others and so mark stiffly – how can the courses be completely fair?

Teachers are provided with resource packs for use in preparing coursework, together with examples of candidates' work from previous examinations to demonstrate the standards required. There are also opportunities to talk with other teachers and moderators from the awarding bodies at meetings, in order to standardise work from the current examination.

What is a moderator?

The moderator is somebody outside your school who will look at the work of your class in relation to the coursework done by other schools. If the moderator thinks your teacher has marked too harshly or too leniently, compared with other teachers, then the marks will be adjusted to bring them into line. So the system is doubly fair because more than one person will be marking your work.

Will I know what marks I get for my coursework?

Your school might tell you how well you have done in individual pieces of work, but you are unlikely to be told your overall coursework mark – after all, the moderator system may see it changed.

5. THE EXAM UNDER EXAMINATION

After you've put in all the hard work over two years, what about the last hurdle – the exam itself?

Probably the greatest difference between school examinations and the GCSE examinations is time. In most schools the end-of-year exams are concentrated into approximately two weeks, maybe less. This is possible because most schools do not offer a very large number of subjects. So the exams come thick and fast, often two or three in a day.

It's very different with the GCSE. Exams are spread over a much longer period of time – so you should find that your exams are well spaced out, with free days in between. Great – more time for revision! But then you may need more time because you'll be tested on two years' work. The timetable for exams is drawn up well in advance, so you should know the term before the exams start when you will actually sit each paper.

When I come to take my exams, will subjects clash on the timetable?

Each year the awarding bodies get together and draw up a common timetable to avoid possible clashes of exams for students taking subjects from different bodies.

Will we really *all* do the same exam papers?

No. In most cases students sit different papers, appropriate to their individual ability level. This process is known as 'tiering' and most large-entry GCSE subjects are examined through a foundation tier covering grades C to G and a higher, overlapping tier covering grades A* to D. In this higher tier, though, students entered for the higher grade are occasionally 'marked down' to an E grade.

For each tier of entry, the written question papers will:

- be at an appropriate level of difficulty for the range of grades available at that tier
- encourage the more able to respond at a greater depth
- provide opportunities for the less able to show what they know
- use appropriate language.

In Maths there are *three* overlapping tiers and separate content is specified in the syllabuses for each tier of entry. The highest tier includes material targeted at candidates expected to achieve grades A* to B, but grade C is still available for students who perform less well than expected. The intermediate tier includes more material targeted at candidates expected to achieve grades B and C, with grades D and E also available. The foundation tier covers grades D to G.

Art, History, Music, Physical Education and Religious Studies are not tiered. In these subjects questions can be set that allow all students to respond effectively at their own level. Examination papers are therefore designed to cover the full grade range, without the need for tiering.

Are short courses tiered?

Yes. The tiering arrangements for GCSE short courses are the same as those for the full GCSEs in the same subject.

Remember that coursework is another way of enabling candidates to demonstrate different levels of ability. Coursework has the additional advantages of a less pressured environment and the availability of guidance from a teacher.

Do I have a say in which tier I am entered for?

It's your subject teacher who is responsible for deciding which tier of entry will give you the best opportunity to achieve your best possible grade. The decisions are usually made around January in the year of the exam. The teacher will certainly consider how well you have been doing in this subject, along with the result of any mock exam. If you are not happy with the decision about GCSE entry your parents or guardians have the right to discuss the issue with the head teacher.

It all sound a bit complicated to me!

If it sounds a complicated system, don't worry. Before you get anywhere near taking the exams your teachers will tell you which kind of paper you will be taking in each subject. They will also probably show you examples of what the exam papers will look like and you'll have a chance to try them out. You'll be in no doubt about what to do, and what's expected of you, when you take the exam.

I just can't do exams, I go to pieces. Is there any hope for me?

The good news is that the GCSE does help people like you. If you choose the subjects that best suit you, work consistently at your coursework and then revise thoroughly for the final examination, you should do well.

Will the GCSE give me a fair deal?

Most people think so, and here are the reasons why:

- It is fair because it tests all your skills.
- The courses are interesting and relevant.
- Everybody has the same chance of success because you all take the same exam and succeed at your own level.

6. CHOOSING THE RIGHT SUBJECTS

Subjects that can be taken at GCSE (as full courses) in England and Wales

Accounting
Agriculture and Horticulture
Archaeology
Arabic
Art
Art: Ceramics
Art: Craft Studies
Art: Critical and Historical Studies
Art: Drawing and Painting
Art: Graphics
Art: Photography
Art: Printmaking
Art: Sculpture
Art: Textiles
Art: Three Dimensional Studies
Astronomy

Bengali
Biblical Hebrew
Business Studies
Business & Communications
  Studies
Business Studies and Economics

Catering
Chinese
Classical Civilisation
Communication Studies

Design & Technology
Design & Technology and Art
Design & Technology and
  Business Studies
Design & Technology and Catering

Design & Technology and
  Electronics
Design & Technology and
  Information Technology
Design & Technology: Automotive
  Studies
Design & Technology: Electronic
  Products
Design & Technology: Electronic
  Products and Business Studies
Design & Technology: Food
  Technology
Design & Technology: Food
  Technology and Business
  Studies
Design & Technology: Graphic
  Products
Design & Technology: Graphic
  Products and Business
  Studies
Design & Technology: Industrial
  Production
Design & Technology: Resistant
  Materials Technology
Design & Technology: Resistant
  Materials Technology and
  Business Studies
Design & Technology: Systems &
  Control Technology
Design & Technology: Systems &
  Control Technology and
  Business Studies
Design & Technology: Textile
  Technology

Design & Technology: Textile
Technology and Business
Studies
Dutch
Drama
Drama and Theatre Arts

Economics
Electronics
English
English Literature
Environmental Studies
Expressive Arts

French
French and Business Studies

General Studies
Geography
Geography and Business Studies
Geography and History
German
German and Business Studies
Greek (Classical)
Gujarati

Health Studies
History
Home Economics: Child
Development
Home Economics: Consumer
Studies
Home Economics: Food and
Nutrition
Home Economics: Textiles
Humanities

Information Studies
Information & Communication
Technology
Information & Communication
Technology and Business Studies
Italian

Japanese

Latin
Law

Mathematics
Media Studies
Modern Greek
Modern Hebrew
Music

Nautical Studies

Office Applications

Panjabi
Performance Arts: Dance
Persian
Physical Education
Polish
Politics
Portuguese
Psychology

Religious Studies
Russian

Science: Biology
Science: Chemistry
Science: Double Award
Science: Geology
Science: Human Physiology and
Health
Science: Physics
Science: Rural
Science: Single Award
Social Science
Sociology
Spanish
Spanish and Business Studies
Statistics

Travel & Tourism   Welsh
Turkish   Welsh Literature
                                   Welsh Second Language
Urdu

How to choose the right subjects

Because young people frequently change their career ideas at this stage, most schools put some restrictions on your choice of subject. The National Curriculum ensures that you keep your options open by avoiding narrow specialisation too early.

The National Curriculum limits the number of choices that have to be made by young people during Year 9 (Year 10 in Northern Ireland), but when there are still choices to be made, how should you set about choosing?

1. *Ask yourself:*
   What do I want to do when I leave school?
   (a) If you know exactly what career you want to follow then turn to Chapter 9 and see what GCSE subjects are required.
   (b) If you are thinking of studying for a degree eventually then take a look at a couple of publications that are likely to be available in your school or college careers library. *The Big UCAS Guide to University and College Entrance* is the official guide published by the Universities and Colleges Admissions Service, while *The Complete Degree Course Offers for Entry into Higher Education* by Brian Heap is also available on CD-ROM. These excellent guides give all the essential information about the choice of higher education, including details of the subjects required for different higher education courses. In addition, ECCTIS (*www.ecctis.co.uk*) produces a computer database of full- and part-time further and higher education courses.
   (c) If you've no idea at this stage, don't worry. You are probably in the majority . . . 13 or 14 is rather early for most people to decide on a career. Your aim now should be to choose a selection of subjects that will keep as many career doors open as possible.

2. *What am I good at? and What do I enjoy doing?*
   Are any of the available GCSE subjects closely related to these interests?
   Make sure you find out as much as you can about the content of the GCSE courses that are options for you. Just to take one example, the criteria for History have recently been changed and now require syllabuses to include 25% British history.
   Now add any subjects you think are essential to your chosen career. Already you are beginning to get a list.

3. *Which subjects are most likely to be on offer at my school?*
   Here is a list of the subjects most likely to be offered by schools.

MATHS	HUMANITIES
ENGLISH	Geography
Language	History
Literature	Religious Education
SCIENCES	EXPRESSIVE ARTS
Biology	Art
Chemistry	Dance
Physics	Drama
Science – Single or Double Award	Music
TECHNOLOGY	MODERN LANGUAGES
Business Studies	French
Design & Technology	German
Information Technology	Spanish

4. *What about other options?*
   Before you make your final choice, remember – the GCSE offers a range of subjects you've probably never tried before. Many schools will organise a few sample lessons in the 'new' subjects they offer, to give you some idea of what they are like. These subjects could be useful, even decisive for your future career, so give them serious consideration.
   You may still have a rather long list, so the next question must be:

5. *How many subjects should I take?*
   As many as you are capable of doing well. It is better to get a C or D grade in six subjects than a G in nine. It is well worth listening to the advice of your teachers about getting the balance right.

Coursework overload

Don't overburden yourself with coursework.
   Some subjects involve more research-based coursework to be done outside the classroom. History and Geography are examples of this. Maths and Modern Foreign Languages, on the other hand, will probably include relatively little. As it is important to make sure you have sufficient time to do every project well, make sure you get the workload right by *not* picking too many subjects that are heavy on coursework. So, check coursework content with your teachers.

What are modular courses?

Modular schemes offer students the opportunity to study relatively small parts of the curriculum in a concentrated period. Each unit or module contains very specific and easily understood learning targets, with student learning assessed at the end of each module.

The different structure of modular courses, with a heavy emphasis on assessment and systematic feedback between teacher and student, suits some students better than the more traditional structure.

In most subjects except Design & Technology at least 60% of the marks will still come from terminal examinations. In addition, end-of-unit tests that count towards the final assessment will be set and marked externally; and any marks allocated for coursework will be set at the same limit as for the ordinary GCSE in that subject.

And finally . . .

Your teachers will see it as part of their responsibility to ensure that you are entered for the most appropriate subjects and syllabuses available. So, before opting for, or committing yourself to, any course, make sure that you ask each subject teacher:

- how much reading is involved;
- how much writing is involved;
- how much coursework is involved;
- what percentage of the marks is given for coursework;
- if there's the option of different tiers of assessment;
- if there's an oral test;
- if you'll have to gather information for yourself;
- if projects are involved;
- what practical skills are involved;
- how much laboratory or fieldwork is involved.

With this information you should be well placed to begin to make your GCSE decisions.

7. THE VOCATIONAL ALTERNATIVE

What is GNVQ?

GNVQ stands for General National Vocational Qualification. GNVQ courses are intended to provide you with the knowledge, skills and understanding you need for work in a broad vocational area. Students are expected to acquire the basic skills and knowledge relevant to the particular vocational area. GNVQs do not provide training for a specific job.

The courses are offered at Foundation, Intermediate and Advanced levels (although the Advanced level is not available at Key Stage 4).

In addition to acquiring the basic skills and a body of knowledge relevant to one of the vocational areas, all students are expected to develop a range of Key Skills. There are six Key Skills – Communication, Application of Number, Information Technology, Working with Others, Improving Own Learning and Performance, and Problem Solving. Three of the Key Skills are mandatory in all GNVQs: Communication, Application of Number and Information Technology. There has also been some trialling of the accreditation of the Key Skill units in Working with Others and Improving Own Learning and Performance.

But how does GNVQ fit in at Key Stage 4?

In recent years GNVQ has become the main alternative vocational pathway at KS4. The aim is to assist progression into a vocational route post-16 and provide a foundation for further education and/or training within the National Vocational Qualification (NVQ) framework.

GNVQs continue to be available in a revised form from September 2000.

There are several ways in which you may have some involvement with GNVQs at KS4. These all complement the National Curriculum – and remember that all students must take the GCSE or equivalent in Maths, English and Science – and can help provide a more appropriate route for some students.

You may be able to take:

- a GNVQ Part One
- GNVQ units, or
- a full GNVQ, or
- a GNVQ Language unit or IT unit instead of a GCSE short course.

What is Part One GNVQ?

It is a curriculum framework that enables students to combine GCSE (or a vocational qualification equivalent to GCSE) in the compulsory subjects with other National Curriculum subjects and other subjects or courses that lead to vocational qualifications.

Part One itself was designed to take 20% of the curriculum time in KS4. It offers a package of GNVQ units (or modules). Part One is available at two levels:

- at Foundation level – broadly equivalent to two GCSEs at grades D–G;
- at Intermediate level – equivalent to two GCSEs at grades A*–C.

Courses at both levels have three units and take twice as much time as a GCSE course. Much of the work that students do during the course goes towards building a portfolio that counts for two-thirds of the final grade. Students also have to pass a test on each unit. The tests can be taken during the course or at the end. The qualification is graded pass, credit or distinction at each level.

Part One results feature in school performance tables.

What subjects are available at Part One?

Part One GNVQ is available in seven subjects:

Art & Design
Business
Engineering
Health & Social Care
ICT
Leisure & Tourism
Manufacturing

A Part One GNVQ is made up of three units from the six-unit GNVQ at the same level. The chosen subject is usually taken over the two-year period of KS4. As well as the three vocational units, the course contains three units in the mandatory Key Skills of Communication, Application of Number and Information Technology. To take the example of a Part One in Business at Intermediate level, the three vocational units are:

- Business organisations and employment
- Students in business organisations
- Consumers and customers.

With all GNVQs each unit sets out clearly what learning students must cover to produce the assessment evidence required.

The flexibility of the unit structure means that some students continue their GNVQ studies post-16, in order to complete the full GNVQ qualification.

Can you tell me a bit more about the key skills?

As mentioned above, all GNVQ candidates have to produce evidence of achievement in Key Skills in Communication, Application of Number and Information Technology. The intention is to encourage a more integrated approach to the teaching of such skills across subject boundaries. For example, revision of the National Curriculum Subject Orders has taken account of GNVQ Key Skill requirements. So GCSE English contributes to Key Skill Communication and GCSE Maths to Key Skill Application of Number. The National Curriculum programme of study for ICT (whether taken as a GCSE course or not) makes a similar contribution to the Key Skill Information Technology.

The other Key Skills – Improving Own Learning and Performance, Working with Others and Problem Solving – are not formally accredited on the final award. But all GNVQ candidates have regular practice in them, just as they do with the mandatory Key Skill units. All Key Skills are acquired in a work-related context and this is one aspect of GNVQs that makes them attractive to employers.

You should see Key Skills as an important part of your education throughout Key Stage 4 and beyond. A new Key Skills award for post-16 students was introduced in September 2000. GCSE passes will partially qualify students for the new award and it is intended that the new qualification will be available from GCSE to degree level – at National Curriculum levels 1–4. The new qualification is designed to be taken by all young people aged 16–19, whether they are in school, college, work-based training or employment.

From the year 2002 points for university entrance will also be given for Key Skills, as they will be for national vocational qualifications (the points system was previously based mainly on A-level achievement).

Each of the three main Key Skills will be assessed through both a portfolio and an external test. Students who get at least a C in a GCSE in ICT will automatically get a new qualification – a level 2 Key Skills unit – worth 10 UCAS points, or $\frac{1}{12}$th of an A-level A grade. English and Maths GCSE candidates can also earn these points if they submit an extra portfolio.

Achievement at level 3 in all three Key Skills will be worth 60 points, the same as a grade A at AS level. However, the Key Skills points are likely to be added up separately from the A-level points and then used as a secondary guide for university admissions tutors.

Remember that students taking Part One at KS4 must still follow the National Curriculum in English, Maths, Science, Physical Education, Technology and a Modern Foreign Language. Part One GNVQs in Engineering and Manufacturing meet National Curriculum requirements in Design & Technology. GNVQ study in ICT meets National Curriculum requirements and IT Key Skills requirements. Like other students, Part One students also follow programmes that include Religious Education, Sex Education and Careers Education.

How are GNVQs assessed?

Students starting one-year or two-year Part One GNVQ courses in 2000 or 2001 will be assessed on the current model. Awards are made at pass, merit and distinction grades.

The assessment for Part One GNVQ courses consists of four elements:

- a portfolio containing students' work in the three vocational units, assessed by teachers and checked both within the school and by the awarding body;
- evidence of attainment in the Key Skills, with teachers' assessments checked both within the school and by the awarding body;
- end-of-unit tests, set and marked by the awarding body, checking the coverage of the knowledge requirements of each vocational unit (there is a single resit opportunity for the external tests);
- extension tests checking depth of understanding for students aiming at the high grades of merit or distinction.

The weighting for assessment is two-thirds internal to one-third external, which is the common pattern for most GNVQ study.

From September 2002 the lower levels of the GNVQ will be replaced by the new 'vocational GCSE' in a range of subjects (possibly including Manufacturing, IT, Health Care, Engineering, Art & Design, and Catering). So students starting courses in 2002 will be aiming for the new vocational GCSE qualifications, which are expected to fit broadly into the standard GCSE assessment framework. The QCA is working with ACCAC and CCEA on the technical aspects of applying GCSE grading to the new vocational qualifications.

Can I be sure that GNVQs are as high a standard as GCSEs?

GNVQs meet strict standards approved by the QCA, the body responsible for monitoring the examination process and ensuring that awarding bodies meet the national requirements.

Part One teaching and learning opportunities are particularly strong in encouraging students to:

- assume responsibility for their own learning
- meet deadlines
- manage their time effectively
- take the initiative in organising their work.

Where does Part One lead?

The Part One qualification offers several different progression routes:

- adding the three further units needed to complete the full GNVQ at the same level;
- moving up to the next level, ie from Foundation to Intermediate or from Intermediate to Advanced;
- taking A-level and/or AS courses;
- following a mixed programme, eg combining GCSEs or A-levels with a vocational or occupational course;
- going into employment;
- going on to further, more occupationally specific training, eg working towards NVQs (usually from the base of a job or traineeship).

How else can I be involved in GNVQs at Key Stage 4?

The other options that involve GNVQ or NVQ include:

1. *Taking a full, six-unit GNVQ at Intermediate or Foundation level.* This would mean that there would be no time for subjects outside the mandatory curriculum, as it would take up 30–40% of curriculum time. This is not an attractive alternative for many schools, concerned with their position in the performance tables published annually by the government. However, Foundation level is formally accepted as being the equivalent to four GCSEs at grades D–G, while Intermediate level is equivalent to four GCSEs at grades A*–C.
2. *GNVQ units.* In some schools students will be able to take a specific GNVQ unit. Unit credits gained in this way can count towards a full GNVQ taken at a later stage. However, at present unit certification does not feature in school performance tables.
3. *NVQ or units towards an NVQ.* NVQs are mainly intended for young people and adults doing particular jobs in specific areas. At KS4 some students may earn these qualifications through taking on a regular work placement, through a college course, or through working with a training provider. Students gain a certificate for each unit as they complete

it. When students are ready an assessor checks that they can demonstrate the knowledge, skills and understanding that they will need in the workplace, to do the tasks that are covered by the particular unit. At age 14–16 students will be working towards NVQs (or units of them) at level 1 or level 2. Level 1 is the equivalent to GCSE grades D–G, while level 2 is the equivalent to GCSE grades A*–C.

What about vocational GCSEs?

As mentioned above, in 2002 the government plans to introduce vocational courses to replace Foundation, Intermediate and Part One GNVQs. Vocational GCSEs will retain the distinctive features of a GNVQ – a strong portfolio basis and a specific vocational or occupational focus. The courses will have the same status as other GCSEs.

Ministers have asked QCA to work with ACCAC and CCEA to consult with schools and colleges on the range of subjects currently on offer and also on the issues of assessment.

8. BEFORE YOU MAKE UP YOUR MIND

Before you make your final selection, here are a few more questions that might occur to you.

Are all the GCSE subjects recognised by employers, professional bodies, universities and colleges of further education?

The honest answer is 'no'. If a minimum number of GCSEs is required of students, these institutions (or individual admissions tutors or their departments) will sometimes not accept creative and expressive subjects such as Art and Music.

The advice is: *CHECK YOUR OPTIONS ARE SUITABLE FOR YOUR LONG-TERM PLANS.*

But don't get the idea that subjects such as Art and Music are not good courses to take. They are. It depends on what you want to do. For example, if you are thinking of becoming a graphic designer or an architect, then you should take Art. And that is quite apart from the value of such subjects in helping you develop a broader range of personal skills and interests.

Why do employers and colleges often ask for five subjects all taken at one time?

By asking for five subjects at one sitting employers can expect you to be capable of coping with a lot of sustained work. It gives them a better idea of your all-round ability.

What are 'academic' subjects?

You'll hear students use the term 'academic subjects'. They are referring to subjects that are considered to involve theoretical work rather than practical skills. This distinction is no longer a helpful one, since it creates an artificial divide between the so-called 'academic' subjects and the practical and 'vocational' courses. GCSE has put increasing emphasis on relevance and practical skills, while most of the subjects labelled 'practical' or 'vocational' are intellectually demanding in at least some of their components.

What can I do if the GCSE subject I want to do is not offered at my school?

The best advice is to wait until you are 16, when you'll probably be able to find it at a college, where the range of subjects offered is sometimes wider. In fact, many sixth form teachers and tutors suggest students take an additional GCSE as well as A-levels or other courses they may be taking. If, however, you want to take the subject before then, you may be able to find a specialist tutor, although this will not always be easy.

Can you get the top grade in all subjects?

Yes, but only if your syllabuses have been designed to include all the work necessary for the top grade or level to be awarded. If it is more appropriate to your needs, the syllabus in some subjects may be designed so that the work involved will earn, at the highest, a grade C. Similarly, it is possible for syllabuses to be designed so that the lowest level that can be awarded for the work involved is a grade E: see the paragraphs on tiering in Chapter 5.

Your teacher would tell you if a course you will be doing involves all the work required for the top level awards or if it is restricted in some way.

It is also important to remember that if you opt for an exam on high-level papers with, say, grade C as the lowest level available, you are *not* guaranteed that minimum. If you fail to achieve that minimum standard, you will be UNGRADED. In a typical year approximately 5% of candidates entered for the higher tier may not score sufficient marks to reach the minimum standard for grade D and are therefore unclassified.

Why do I have to start selecting my GCSE subjects so early in Year 9 (Year 10 in Northern Ireland)?

A large school might well have over 200 students in one year, choosing from quite a few different subjects. Drawing up a timetable to suit everyone, including the students and the teachers, is a major task. These days most schools make at least some use of a computer, but it still takes time.

9. CHOOSING THE RIGHT GCSEs FOR YOUR CAREER

This chapter will tell you the GCSEs you should consider studying if you have a certain career, or possibly several careers, in mind.

In 1999 a government-sponsored MORI opinion poll found that fewer than a third of GCSE students picked subjects because they liked them. Less than half allowed their academic strengths to influence their decisions. In by far the most cases subjects were chosen to help job prospects.

There are different ways of getting into many careers – but the usual method for most careers, and the *only* way for many, is through a RECOGNISED TRAINING COURSE or a DEGREE, PROFESSIONAL or OTHER COURSE.

There are other less rigid forms of entry to some careers, and you will always hear about students who have succeeded in different walks of life without qualifications. But they are the exceptions. For the vast majority of us the only way is through qualifications.

To check the qualifications you will need, this is what you do:

- Look up all the careers that interest you.
- Write down all the GCSE subjects required.
- Make a list of all the different subjects mentioned.

This will give you a good base on which to build your choice of subject. You should do further research in your school careers library and/or in your local careers centre library. The books and leaflets there will probably be filed under the Careers Library Classification Index (CLCI). We have included the CLCI reference for each job in our listings, but your careers teacher, careers adviser or personal adviser will give you any help you need in finding your way around the library. Other booklets and leaflets that may help you to find out more about careers and courses at this stage include:

- *Occupations* (COIC)
- *Working in . . .* series of booklets (COIC)
- *Directory of Further Education.*

and don't forget the range of computer programs that help you look at your interests and abilities. Some of them also produce a list of possible jobs linked to those interests and abilities. You may already have tried one of these programs but, if not, ask if they are available in your school or at the local careers office. They include:

- CID (Careers Information Database)
- Odyssey
- KUDOS.

The information given for each occupation in the following section is as follows:

Job title

Minimum entry level

Within the National Qualifications framework all qualifications fit in at one of six levels from the basic Entry Level (Level 0) to Level 5. Our tables indicate the minimum level at which you can reasonably expect to enter each particular career.

Essential GCSEs

This column indicates which subjects you should definitely be offering at GCSE (and remember that a higher grade (A*–C) will often be required.

Useful subjects

Those subjects where GCSE courses (or sometimes other qualifications, such as Part One GNVQ) are valuable.

CLCI reference

The final column gives the Careers Library Classification Index reference for each job in our listings.

In Scotland

As well as the different qualifications structure, there are also different career structures for some professions in Scotland. As a consequence, Scottish readers (or those anticipating a career in Scotland) are advised to seek more detailed information where it seems appropriate.

I'm Thinking About a Career in . . . Administration or Office Work

Job title	Minimum entry level	Essential GCSEs	Useful subjects	Other academic/training requirements	CLCI reference
Administrative/Business Management Trainee	3	English, Maths	Business, Geography, ICT, Language, Science	Variety of routes: eg business course after GCSEs or A-levels, direct entry after A-levels or degree	CAL/CAP
Bilingual Secretary	3	English, Language (preferably 2)	Business, Geography, ICT, Maths	A-level in at least 1 modern language at higher levels; bilingual secretarial course after GCSEs, A-levels or degree	CAT
Civil Service Administrative Assistant/Officer	2	English	Business, Geography, History, ICT, Maths	None before entry	CAB
Clerk/Clerical Assistant	1		English, ICT, Maths	Office NVQ training or direct entry	CAT
Company Secretary	3	English, Maths	Business, ICT	2 A-levels or BTEC National Diploma/Certificate/SVQ2 or degree	CAP
Environmental Health Officer	3	English, Maths, Science	ICT	A-levels (including at least 1 Science), then degree or diploma in Environmental Health	COP

Job title	Minimum entry level	Essential GCSEs	Useful subjects	Other academic/training requirements	CLCI reference
Executive Officer (Civil Service)	3	English, Maths	Business, Geography, History, ICT, Language	2 A-levels or degree	CAB
Health & Safety Inspector	4	English, Maths, Science	ICT	A-levels (often in Science), followed by a degree or HNC/HND in a scientific or technological subject	COT
Local Government Administrator	2	English, Maths	Business, ICT	Variety of routes: often at graduate level, but also after GCSEs or A-levels	CAG
Local Government Clerk	2	English, Maths	Business, ICT	None before entry	CAG
Personnel Officer	3	English, Maths	Business, ICT	2 A-levels and often a degree	CAS
Receptionist	1	English	ICT, Language, Maths	Office NVQ training or receptionist course is an advantage	CAT
Secretary/Personal Assistant	1	English	Business, ICT, Language, Maths	Secretarial course after GCSEs or A-levels	CAT

Career					
Specialist Secretary (eg Legal, Medical)	3	English, Maths	Business, ICT	Secretarial course (preferably a specialist course) after GCSEs or A-levels	CAL/ LAZ/ CAT
Tax Inspector	4	English, Maths	ICT	A-levels and degree	CAB
Telephonist	1	English	ICT, Language	None before entry, but office NVQ training may be an advantage	CAT
Trading Standards Officer	3	English, Maths, Science	Business, Design & Technology, ICT	A-levels (Science may be preferred) or equivalent; often graduate entry	COP
Typist/Word Processor Operator	1	English, Maths	ICT	Keyboard skills – through school or college course	CAT

Useful website

Local government – www.lgcareers.com

I'm Thinking About a Career in ... Agriculture, Forestry or Horticulture

Job title	Minimum entry level	Essential GCSEs	Useful subjects	Other academic/training requirements	CLCI reference
Farm Manager	3/4	4 including English, Maths, Science	Business Studies	Diploma, A-levels, degree	WAB
Farm Worker	Entry/1		English, Maths, Science, practical subjects		WAB
Fish Farmer	2/3/4	4 including Double Science		Diploma, Science A-levels, degree	WAH
Fisherman	Entry/1	No special requirements	Geography, Nautical Studies	None before entry	WAH
Forest Officer	3/4	4 including English, Maths, Science	Environmental Science, Geography	Environmental Science, Diploma, Forestry Degree (after Science A-levels)	WAF
Forest Worker	Entry/1		Science, practical subjects		WAF
Gamekeeper	Entry/1		Sciences (for Biology, Rural Science and Environmental Science content), practical subjects		WAM

Gardener	Entry/1		Sciences (for Biology, Rural Science and Environmental Science content)		WAD
Horticultural Manager	3/4	4 including English, Maths, Science	Business Studies, Geography	National Diploma, Higher National Diploma, degree	WAD/WAB
Horticultural Worker	Entry/1/2		Science subjects		WAD
Landscape Architect	4	5 including English, Maths/Science, History/Geography/Modern Foreign Language	Art, Biology, Botany, Design & Technology, Environmental Science, Geology	Diploma/degree in Landscape Architecture	UL
Park Keeper/Grounds Staff	Entry/1		Sciences		WAD

Useful websites

Horticulture – www.horticulture.demon.co.uk
Land-based industries – www.lantra.co.uk

I'm Thinking About a Career . . . Working with Animals

Job title	Minimum entry level	Essential GCSEs	Useful subjects	Other academic/training requirements	CLCI reference
Blacksmith	Entry/1		Maths, Design & Technology, Engineering, Science, practical subjects	None before entry	SAW
Groom/Stablehand	Entry/1/2	If you have some GCSEs, you may take equestrian exams	Science/Biology	None before entry	WAM
Horse Riding Instructor	Entry/1/2	4 including English	Science/Biology	None before entry	WAM
Kennel Worker	Entry/1	An advantage	Science/Biology	None before entry	WAM
Veterinary Nurse	1/2	4 including English Language and Maths or Science to qualify for the Royal College of Veterinary Surgeons Veterinary Nursing Scheme	Science/Biology		WAL

Veterinary Surgeon	4	Good spread	English, Maths, Double Science (or equivalent)	Veterinary degree is essential – this requires very good science A-levels	WAL
Zoo Keeper	Entry/1/2	No set requirements, but good GCSEs helpful	English, Maths, Science, Geography, a foreign language, practical subjects	None before entry	WAM

Useful websites

Careers with horses – www.equiworld.net/abrs
www.bhs.org.uk

Veterinary Surgeon – www.rcvs.org.uk

I'm Thinking About a Career . . . in the Armed Forces

Job title	Minimum entry level	Essential GCSEs	Useful subjects	Other academic/training requirements	CLCI reference
Army – Soldiers and Service Women	Entry/1/2		Maths, Science, Design & Technology	None before entry	BAF
Army Officer	2/3/4	5	English, Maths and Science or a Modern Foreign Language	Most opportunities require at least 2 A-levels and/or a degree	B/BAF
RAF Airman/Woman	Entry/1/2	Maths, Science and preferably English	Sciences	None before entry	BAL
RAF Officer	3/4	Minimum of 5 including English Language and Maths	Science	A-levels and/or higher diploma/degree	B/BAL
Royal Marines – Other Ranks	Entry/1/2		Selection test involves reasoning, English Language, Numeracy and mechanical comprehension	None before entry	BAB

Royal Navy/WRNS Ratings	Entry/1/2	Technical specialisms require 1, 2 or more including English, Maths and a Science. Medical technicians require 5	Scientific and technical/practical subjects	None before entry	BAB
Royal Navy and Royal Marines Officer	2/3/4	5 including English and Maths	Science, Languages	A-levels normally required; graduate entry also available	B/BAB

Useful websites

Army – www.army.mod.uk
RAF – www.raf.mod.uk
Royal Navy and Marines – www.royal-navy.mod.uk

I'm Thinking About a Career . . . in Art and Design

Job title	Minimum entry level	Essential GCSEs	Useful subjects	Other academic/training requirements	CLCI reference
Art Teacher	4	5 including English, Maths and Art	Design & Technology	A-levels, Foundation Art course, BEd or art degree, postgraduate teacher training	FAB
Artist	3/4	3–5 for formal training	Art, any craft subject	Art training after GCSE or A-levels	E
Designer (Graphic, Fashion, Furniture, Interior etc)	3/4	3–5	Art & Design, English, subject appropriate to specialism, eg crafts, textiles/dress etc; Art portfolio	BTEC Diploma or Degree in Art & Design after Foundation Course and/ or A-levels	ED EJ SAJ ET
Display Dresser	Entry/1/2	No set requirements, but good GCSEs helpful	Art, practical/ craft subjects	Art or design course	ET
Florist	1/2	3 including English, Maths and Science	Science, Art & Design, practical subjects	Usually Modern Apprenticeship/NVQ training	OFM
Graphic Designer/ Illustrator	3/4	4–5 including English and Science	Design & Technology, Art	Specialist training after GCSEs or Foundation Course and/or A-levels	ED

Museum/Art Gallery Curator	4	English, Art and Modern Foreign Language	Classical and/or Modern Languages, History, Design & Technology, Textiles, Science for specialist collections	Degree in Fine Art or Art History; postgraduate or research experience	FAE
Photographer	1/2/3/4	4	English, Science or Maths, Art, Photography	NVQ trainings available after GCSEs or A-level	EV
Press Photographer	2/4	5 including English	Art, Photography, Sciences		FAC

Useful websites

Art and Design – design-council.org.uk
Museum/Art Gallery Curator – www.chnto.co.uk/training/index.html
Press Photographer – www.itecharlow.co.uk/nctj

I'm Thinking About a Career Working With . . . Children or Young People

Job title	Minimum entry level	Essential GCSEs	Useful subjects	Other academic/training requirements	CLCI reference
Care Assistant	Entry/1/2/3		Home Economics, English, Social Sciences	Care/Social Work course, NVQ training	KEB
Careers Officer/Adviser	4	5 including English	Social Sciences	A-levels, degree, diploma	KED
Educational Psychologist	4	Maths, English	Science, Social Sciences, Statistics	A-levels, Psychology degree, teaching requirements	KEL
Nursery Nurse	3	2–3 including English	Home Economics, Music, Crafts, Science, Social Sciences	NNEB course, A-levels	KEB
Residential Social Worker	4	4–5 including English	Social Sciences	A-levels, Diploma in Social Work	KEB
Teacher	4	3 including English, Maths		A-levels, degree, Teacher Training/BEd degree	FAB
Youth and Community Worker	4	5 including English	Social Sciences	A-levels, diploma, degree	KEG

Useful websites

Educational Psychologist – www.bps.org.uk
Social Work – www.ccetsw.org.uk

I'm Thinking About a Career . . . in Computing

Job title	Minimum entry level	Essential GCSEs	Useful subjects	Other academic/training requirements	CLCI reference
Applications Programmer	2/3/4	5 including English, Maths, science subjects	ICT, Electronics/ Design & Technology	A-level, diploma, degree	CAV
Computer Service Technician	2/3/4	4–5 including English, Maths	ICT	BTEC awards at National or Higher National level/SVQ2 or 3 in Computer Studies, degree	CAV
Microelectronics Engineer	4	English, Maths, Science	Design & Technology/ Engineering, Electronics	A-levels (Maths, Physics, Computer Science), degree in Electronic Engineering	RAL
Systems Analyst	4	English, Maths	Business Studies, ICT	A-levels, degree or BTEC Higher National Award/ SVQ3	CAV
Systems Programmer/ Software Engineer	3/4	English, Maths, Science	Design & Technology/ engineering subjects, Electronics	A-levels (Maths, Science), degree in Maths, Computer Science, Electronic Engineering, BTEC/ SVQ Awards	CAV

Useful websites

Electronic and Software Services – www.e-businessnto.org.uk

I'm Thinking About a Career ... in Construction and Land Services

Job title	Minimum entry level	Essential GCSEs	Useful subjects	Other academic/training requirements	CLCI reference
Architect	4	English, Maths or Science, Art & Design	Design & Technology, ICT	A-levels, degree in Architecture	UB
Architectural/Surveying Technician	2/3/4	4–5 including Maths, English, Science	Design & Technology, ICT	A-levels or BTEC/SVQ award courses	UB UM
Bricklayer/Carpenter/Plumber/Plasterer	1	Maths, Science, Design & Technology	Practical/craft subjects	Modern Apprenticeship/NVQ training	UF
Builder's Labourer	Entry/1		Practical/craft subjects		UF
Building Surveyor/Building Control Officer	Entry/1	Maths, English	Design & Technology	GCSEs or BTEC/SVQ	UM/UD
Building Technician	2/3	English, Maths, Sciences	Design & Technology, practical subjects	BTEC National Diploma/SVQ2	UD
Building Technologist/Site Manager	4	4–5 including English, Maths and Science	Design & Technology	A-levels, Higher National Diploma or degree in Building	UD

Cartographer	4	2–3 to include subjects from English, Maths, Geography, Art, Design & Technology, Science, Languages	ICT	A-levels or BTEC National Diploma/SVQ2	UT
Cartographic Draughtsman/Woman	2/3/4	2–3 to include subjects from English, Maths, Geography, Art, Design & Technology, Science, Languages	ICT	A-levels or BTEC National Diploma/SVQ2	UT
Electrician	2/3	English, Maths, Science	Design & Technology, practical/craft subjects	Modern Apprenticeship/ NVQ training	RAK UF
Glazier/Roofer/Tiler/ Scaffolder	Entry/1		Maths, Science, craft/ practical subjects	Modern Apprenticeship/ NVQ training	UF
Painter & Decorator	Entry/1	Maths	Practical/craft/art subjects	Modern Apprenticeship/ NVQ training	UF
Surveyor	2/3/4	5 including English and Science	Geography, Geology, Design & Technology	A-levels, Higher National Diploma, degree	UM

Job title	Minimum entry level	Essential GCSEs	Useful subjects	Other academic/training requirements	CLCI reference
Town Planner	4	English, Maths and one of History, Geography, Modern Foreign Language	Science, Statistics, Social Sciences	A-levels or equivalent, then a degree	US
Town Planning Technician	2	4 including English, Maths	Geography, History, Design & Technology, Economics, Science	BTEC/SVQ award	US

Useful websites

Architect – www.architecture.com
Architectural Technologist – www.biat.org.uk
Civil Engineering – www.ice.org.uk
Construction Industry – www.citb.org.uk
Engineering Construction – www.ecitb.org.uk
Surveyor – www.rics.org.uk/careers

I'm Thinking About a Career . . . in Engineering

Job title	Minimum entry level	Essential GCSEs	Useful subjects	Other academic/training requirements	CLCI reference
Chartered Engineer	4	5 including Maths, Science, English	Design & Technology, technical/practical subjects, Modern Foreign Languages	Maths/Science (especially Physics) A-levels (or BTEC/SVQ equivalent), degree in Engineering	RAB
Electrician	2		Maths, Science, Design & Technology, practical/technical subjects	Modern Apprenticeship, NVQ training	RAK/UF
Engineering Craftsman/woman	2	Maths, Science, English	Design & Technology, practical/technical subjects	Modern Apprenticeship/ NVQ training	RAB
Engineering Operative	Entry/1	English, Maths, practical and technical subjects	Science		RAB
Engineering Technician	2/3	3–4 from Maths, English, Science, Design & Technology	Practical subjects	Technician Modern Apprenticeship, BTEC National Diploma/ SVQ2	RAB

Job title	Minimum entry level	Essential GCSEs	Useful subjects	Other academic/training requirements	CLCI reference
Incorporated Engineer	4	5 including English, Maths, Science	Design & Technology technical/practical subjects, ICT, Modern Foreign Languages	Maths, Science (especially Physics) A-levels (or BTEC/SVQ equivalent, plus BTEC Higher National Diploma/SVQ3/part time Higher National Certificate, degree in Engineering	RAB
Motor Mechanic	Entry/1		English, Maths, Science	Modern Apprenticeship NVQ training	RAE
Sheet Metal Worker/Plater	Entry/1	English, Maths, Science	Technical/practical subjects		RON

Useful websites

Automobile Engineer – www.mitc.co.uk
Chemical Engineer – www.icheme.org
Engineering and Engineering Manufacture – www.emta.org.uk
Oil Engineer – www.petroleum.co.uk

I'm Thinking About a Career in . . . Entertainment or Performing

Job title	Minimum entry level	Essential GCSEs	Useful subjects	Other academic/training requirements	CLCI reference
Actor/Actress	Entry/1/2/3/4	5	English Literature, Drama, Music	A-levels, degree	GAB
Box Office Staff	Entry/1	Maths	Office skills		GAB
Cameraman/woman/ Camera Operator	2	3 including English, Maths, Science (Physics)	Technical subjects		GAL
Dancer	Entry/1/2/3/4	5	Music, Drama	A-levels, degree	GAF
Fashion/Photographic Model	Entry/1	3	Drama	London College of Fashion course	OT
Film Editor (TV)	3/4	Maths, Science	Art, Drama	A-levels, film course	GAL
Floor/Stage Manager	1/2/3/4	5	Art, Design & Technology, Drama, English, English Literature	Pre-entry courses, degree	GAT
Lighting Technician (Theatre)	1/2/3	Science, Maths, Design & Technology	Art, Drama	Electrician training, Theatre Lighting course	GAT
Make-up Artist	2/3/4	English, Art	Science, History, Drama	Hairdressing, Beauty Therapy, A-levels	GAL/ GAT
Professional Sportsman/ woman	Entry/1				GAG

Job title	Minimum entry level	Essential GCSEs	Useful subjects	Other academic/training requirements	CLCI reference
Singer/Musician	Entry/1/2/3/4		Music, Drama	Music college training, A-levels	GAD
Sound Technician/ Operator (Film/TV)	2/3/4	3 including English Language, Maths, Science	Technical subjects	BTEC Certificate or Diploma at National or Higher Level, BA Music Tonmeister	GAL
Sports/Leisure Centre Manager	2/3/4	5 including English, Maths	Science, Business Studies	BTEC National, degree	GAJ
Stage Designer	4	Art & design subjects	Drama	Theatre/Stage Design course, A-levels	GAT
Studio Manager (Radio)	4	English, Science	Practical subjects	Experience in sound recording or radio	GAL

Useful websites

Dancer and Performing Arts – www.metier.org.uk
Leisure – www.barzone.co.uk
Singer/Musician – www.ism.org
Sport and Recreation – www.spirito.org.uk
Sports/Leisure Centre Management – www.ilam.co.uk
Stage Technician – www.abtt.org.uk

I'm Thinking About a Career ... in Finance

Job title	Minimum entry level	Essential GCSEs	Useful subjects	Other academic/training requirements	CLCI reference
Accountant (Chartered, Management, Public Service)	2/3/4	5 including Maths, English	Business Studies/Economics, Modern Foreign Languages	A-levels or equivalent, degree	NAB
Accounting Technician	1/2	English, Maths	Business Studies/Economics, ICT		NAB
Actuary	3/4	5 including English, Maths	Statistics, Business Studies/Economics	A-levels or equivalent	NAB
Bank/Building Society/Insurance Clerk	1/2	English, Maths	Modern Languages, Business Studies/Economics, ICT		NAD/NAF/NAG
Banker/Bank or Building Society Manager	2/3/4	English, Maths	Modern Foreign Languages, Business Studies/Economics, ICT	A-levels or degree	NAD/NAF
Insurance Broker/Underwriter	2/3/4	4 including English, Maths	Business Studies/Economics	BTEC National Diploma, A-levels, degree	NAG

Job title	Minimum entry level	Essential GCSEs	Useful subjects	Other academic/training requirements	CLCI reference
Insurance Salesman/woman	2	4 including English, Maths	Business Studies/Economics		NAG
Investment Analyst	4	5 including English, Maths	Statistics, Business Studies/Economics	A-levels or degree	NAL
Stockbroker	2/3/4	5 including English, Maths	Business Studies/Economics, ICT, Modern Languages, Geography, Science	A-levels or degree	NAL

Useful websites

Accountancy – www.icaewmembers.co.uk
Banking and Building Society Work – www.fsnto.org
Insurance – www.cii.co.uk

I'm Thinking About a Career . . . in Health, Medicine or Personal Services

Job title	Minimum entry level	Essential GCSEs	Useful subjects	Other academic/training requirements	CLCI reference
Ambulance Staff	Entry/1	4 including English, Maths, Science			JOC
Beautician/Beauty Therapist	Entry/1/2/3/4	3 including English, Science		College course after GCSEs or A-levels	IK
Chiropodist	3/4	5 including English, Double Science (or equivalent)		2 A-levels (preferably Science) then full-time NVQ training	JAT
Chiropractor	4	5 including English, Double Science		3 A-levels (sciences) then full-time NVQ training	JOD
Dental Hygienist	2/3	5 including English, Language, Science		Experience as dental surgery assistant	JAF
Dental Nurse	Entry/1/2/3	2–4 including English, Science		Full-time course sometimes available	JAF
Dental Technician	2/3	4 including English, Maths, Science	Practical/technical subjects	Possibly full-time course	JAF
Dentist	4	Maths, Double Science (or equivalent), English Language		Science A-levels, Dentistry degree	JAF

Job title	Minimum entry level	Essential GCSEs	Useful subjects	Other academic/training requirements	CLCI reference
Dietitian	4	5 including English, Double Science, Maths	Home Economics/Food Studies	2 A-levels (Chemistry and another Science) or BTEC/National Diploma/Certificate/SVQ2 in Science, degree in Dietetics	JAV
Dispensing Optician	2/3	5 including English, Maths, Science	Practical subjects	Possibly full-time NVQ training	JAL
Doctor	4	English, Maths, Double Science		3 A-levels in Maths/Science subjects, medical degree	JAB
Hairdresser	Entry/1		English, Art, Maths, Science	College course, Modern Apprenticeship/NVQ training	IL
Hospital Nurse	2/3/4	5 including English, Science	Home Economics/Food Studies	A-levels, Pre-Nursing/Health Care course	JAD
Hospital Porter, Operating Department Assistant	Entry/1		English, Maths, Science		JOZ
Medical Technical Officer	2/3/4	4 including English, Maths, Double Science	A-levels (sciences), Higher National Diploma, degree		JOB

	Entry/1			
Nursing Auxiliary				JAD
Occupational Therapist	4	5 including English, Science	2 A-levels (sciences preferred), degree in Occupational Therapy	JAR
Optician	4	5 including English, Maths, Double Science (or equivalent)	2 A-levels (Maths and science subjects) degree in Optometry/Opthalmics	JAL / JAL
Orthoptist	4	5 including English, Maths, Science	2 A-levels (Science), Orthoptics Degree	
Osteopath	4	5 including English, Double Science	2 A-levels (Sciences), full-time NVQ training; qualified doctor to train at London College of Osteopathic Medicine	JOD
Pharmacist	4	Home Economics/ Food Studies, Science	A-levels including Chemistry, Pharmacy degree	JAG
Pharmacy Technician	2	3–4 including English, Maths, Science	Maths, practical subjects	JAG

Job title	Minimum entry level	Essential GCSEs	Useful subjects	Other academic/training requirements	CLCI reference
Physiological Measurement Technician (eg Cardiology, Audiology)	2/3	4 including English, Maths, Double Science	Technical/practical subjects	2 Science A-levels	JOB
Physiotherapist	4	5 including English, Maths, Double Science		2 A-levels including Biology, JAN degree in Physiotherapy	
Radiographer	4	5 including English, Maths, Double Science		2 Science A-levels, degree at School of Radiography	JAP
Speech/Language Therapist	4	5 including English	Maths, Modern Foreign Languages	2 Science A-levels, degree	JAS

Useful websites

Health and Medicine – www.skillset.org
www.nhs.careers.nhs.uk

I'm Thinking About a Career . . . in Home Economics or the Hotel and Catering Industry

Job title	Minimum entry level	Essential GCSEs	Useful subjects	Other academic/training requirements	CLCI reference
Chef/Cook	Entry/1/2		Home Economics/Food Studies, Science, French	Modern Apprenticeship/NVQ training, college course	IC
Domestic Staff	Entry/1		Home Economics/Food Studies	IC	
Fast Food Shop Manager	2/3/4	4 including English, Maths	Home Economics/Food Studies, Business Studies	Business Studies or catering course after A-levels	IC
Home Economist	3/4	3–4 including English, Science	Maths, Home Economics/Food Studies	Diploma/Higher Diploma, degree	ID
Hotel/Catering Manager	3/4	3–4 including English, Maths, Science	Maths, Home Economics/Food Studies, Business Studies, French	Hotel & Catering Management Diploma/Higher Diploma, degree	IB
Hotel/Housekeeper	1/2/3	4 including English, Maths, Science	Maths, Home Economics/Food Studies, Science, Art & Design, Business Studies	Full-time course	IC

Job title	Minimum entry level	Essential GCSEs	Useful subjects	Other academic/training requirements	CLCI reference
Hotel Receptionist	2/3	English, Maths	Modern Foreign Languages, Business Studies, ICT	Office training, Hotel Receptionist course	IC
Kitchen Assistant	Entry/1		Home Economics/ Food Studies		IC
Waiter/Waitress	Entry/1		Home Economics/ Food Studies		IC

Useful website

Hotel and Catering – www.springboarduk.org.uk

I'm Thinking About a Career . . . in Information or a Cultural Profession

Job title	Minimum entry level	Essential GCSEs	Useful subjects	Other academic/training requirements	CLCI reference
Archaeologist	4		English, History, Classical Languages, Science	A-levels, degree	FAH
Archivist	4	English	Modern and Classical Languages, History	A-levels, degree	FAG
Author	Entry/1/2/3/4		English, ICT		FAC
Interpreter/Translator	4	English, 2 Modern Foreign Languages	Classical Languages	Languages degree	FAL
Journalist	2/3/4	5 including English	ICT	A-levels, pre-entry course, degree	FAC
Librarian/Information Officer	4	English, Maths, Modern Foreign Language	ICT	A-levels, degree	FAF
Library Assistant/Information Assistant	2/3	4–5 including English, Maths	ICT	BTEC National Diploma, A-levels	FAF
Museum Assistant	2/3	4 including English	Art/design subjects	A-levels, degree	FAE

Job title	Minimum entry level	Essential GCSEs	Useful subjects	Other academic/training requirements	CLCI reference
Museum Conservation Technician	2/3/4	English	Science, History, craft subjects	A-levels, degree	FAE
Publicity Officer/ Public Relations Officer	4	English		A-levels, degree, training in Journalism	OG OG
Publisher/Editor	3/4	English	Maths, design subjects	A-levels, diploma, degree	FAD

Useful websites

Information Science – www.iis.org.uk
Interpreter/Translator – www.languagesnto.org.uk
Journalism – www.itecharlow.co.uk/nctj
www.newspapersoc.org.uk
Librarian/Information Management – www.la-hq.org.uk/directory/careers.html
Museum, Gallery and Heritage Work – www.chnto.co.uk/training/index.html

I'm Thinking About a Career ... in Law

Job title	Minimum entry level	Essential GCSEs	Useful subjects	Other academic/training requirements	CLCI reference
Barrister	4	5 including English	History, Modern Foreign Languages	Arts/Social Science A-levels, degree	LAB
Barrister's Clerk	2/3/4	4 including English, Maths	ICT		LZ
Legal Executive	2/3	4 including English and academic subjects	Business Studies	A-levels	LAD
Legal Secretary	2/3	3–4 including English	Business Studies, ICT	Secretarial course, A-levels	LAZ
Solicitor	4	5 including English	Modern Foreign Languages, History	Arts/Social Science A-levels, Law degree	LAC

Useful websites

Barrister and Solicitor – www.lawcareers.net
www.lawsociety.net

I'm Thinking About a Career . . . in Manufacturing Industry

Job title	Minimum entry level	Essential GCSEs	Useful subjects	Other academic/training requirements	CLCI reference
Baker	Entry/1/2/3	English, Maths, Science	Home Economics	BTEC National Diploma course	SAC
Factory Worker (skilled)	1	2–3	Maths, Science, Design & Technology/ practical subjects		SAB
Factory Worker (unskilled or semi-skilled)	Entry/1		Practical/craft subjects		SAB
Foundry Worker	Entry		Practical/craft subjects, Design & Technology		SAM
Industrial Technician (eg Polymers, Brewing, Textiles, Photographic)	2	4–5 including English, Maths, Science	Design & Technology/ Engineering, practical subjects, ICT	BTEC National	S/SAN/ SAC/ SAG/EV
Industrial Technologist (eg Printing, Textiles, Food, Packaging)	4	Maths, Science, English		A-levels (Science/Maths), Higher National Diploma, degree	S/SAR/ SAG/ SAP/ QON

			Practical subjects		
Packer	Entry/1				SAB
Printing Worker	2/3	English, Maths, Science	Art, Design & Technology		SAR
Production Manager	3/4	4–5 including English, Maths, Science	Engineering/Design & Technology, ICT, Business Studies/Economics	A-levels, degree (Science/Engineering/Business)	ROD
Sewing Machinist/Milliner Woodworking Machinist/	Entry/1		Home Economics (dress and fabrics)		SAH
Furniture Makers	Entry/1	Maths, Design & Technology	Practical/craft subjects		UF

Useful websites

Engineering Manufacture – www.emta.org.uk
Printing – www.bpif.org.uk

I'm Thinking About a Career . . . in Science

Job title	Minimum entry level	Essential GCSEs	Useful subjects	Other academic/training requirements	CLCI reference
Biologist/Biochemist	3/4	5 including English, Maths, Science	Statistics	Science A-levels, Science degree	QOD
Environmental Scientist/ Ecologist	4	English, Maths, Science	Geography, Geology	Science/Maths A-levels, degree	QOL
Geologist/Geophysicist	4	English, Maths, Science	Engineering/ technology subjects, Geography, Geology	Science/Maths A-levels, degree	QOL
Industrial Chemist/ Food Scientist/ Pharmaceuticals Scientist	3/4	5 including English, Maths, Science	Modern Languages	Science A-levels, Science degree	SAV/ QON
Information Scientist	4	English, Maths, Science, Modern Languages	ICT	A-levels, degree	FAF
Laboratory Technician	2/3	4 including Maths, Science	English, ICT	A-levels, diploma	QOX/ JAX/FAB

Mathematician/Statistician	4	English, Maths	Science, Business Studies/Economics, ICT	Maths A-level(s), degree	QOG/ QOJ
Metallurgist/ Materials Scientist	4	English, Maths, Science	Engineering/ technology subjects	Science/Maths A-levels, Metallurgy/Materials Science degree	QOS
Meteorologist	4	English, Maths, Science	ICT, Astronomy	Science/Maths A-levels, BTEC/SVQ, Physics/ Maths/Meteorology degree	QOL
Physicist/Astronomer/ Astrophysicist	4	English, Maths, Science	Engineering/ technology subjects, Astronomy, ICT	Science/Maths A-levels, degree	QOF
Technical Writer	4	English, Maths, Science	Design/Technology, ICT	A-levels, Science/ Engineering subject degree	FAC

Useful websites

Careers in Chemistry – www.chemsoc.org
Careers in Microbiology – www.socgenmicrobiol.org.uk
Environmental Scientist/Ecologist – www.demon.co.uk/bes
Geologist/Geophysicist – www.geolsoc.org.uk
Metallurgist/Materials Scientist – www.instmat.co.uk
Physics and Engineering in Medicine – www.ipem.org.uk

I'm Thinking About a Career . . . in Security

Job title	Minimum entry level	Essential GCSEs	Useful subjects	Other academic/training requirements	CLCI reference
Fire Fighter/Fire Officer	Entry/1/2	English, Maths, Science	Practical subjects		MAF
Police Officer	Entry/1/2/3/4	4 including English, Maths	Social Sciences	A-levels, degree	MAB
Prison Governor	4	English	Social Sciences	Social Sciences/Psychology A-levels, degree	MAD
Prison Officer	Entry/1/2	English	Social Sciences		MAD

Useful website

Police Work – www.police.uk

I'm Thinking About a Career . . . in Selling, Marketing or Advertising

Job title	Minimum entry level	Essential GCSEs	Useful subjects	Other academic/training requirements	CLCI reference
Advertising Account Executive	3/4	English, Maths	Art/design subjects, Social Sciences, Business Studies/Economics	A-levels, degree	OD
Advertising Copywriter	3/4	5 including English	Art/design subjects, Social Sciences	2 A-levels, diploma, degree	OD
Estate Agent/Auctioneer	2/3/4	4–5 including English, Maths	Science, Business Studies/Economics	A-levels, diploma, degree	UM
Market Research Interviewer	1/2	English, Maths			OB
Marketing Manager	4	4 including English, Maths	Business Studies/ Economics, Modern Languages, Social Sciences	A-levels, Diploma, Business Studies/Marketing degree	OB
Marketing Research Executive	3/4	5 including English, Maths	Business Studies/ Economics, Modern Languages, Science, Statistics, Social Sciences	A-levels, degree	OB

Job title	Minimum entry level	Essential GCSEs	Useful subjects	Other academic/training requirements	CLCI reference
Purchasing/Buying Assistant	2	4–5 including English, Maths	Business Studies/ Economics, ICT		OP
Purchasing Officer/Buyer	2/3/4	4–5 including English, Maths	Business Studies/ Economics, ICT	A-levels, degree, Business Studies qualification	OP
Retail Manager	2/3/4	4–5 including English, Maths	Business Studies/ Economics	A-levels, BTEC/SVQ, degree	OE
Sales Representative/ Manager	1/2	English, Maths		A-levels, degree	OM/OE
Shop Assistant/ Shelf Filler/Cashier	Entry/1	English, Maths			OE
Telephone Sales Clerk	1/2	English, Maths			OM

Useful website

Advertising – www.adassoc.org.uk

I'm Thinking About a Career . . . in Social and Community Services

Job title	Minimum entry level	Essential GCSEs	Useful subjects	Other academic/training requirements	CLCI reference
Charities Manager/ Organiser	3/4	5 including English	Maths, Business Studies, Social Sciences	A-levels, degree, Social Work training	KEM
Health Visitor	2/3/4	5 including English, Maths, Science	Home Economics/ Food Studies, Social Sciences	WRNS Nurse Training, Health Visitor's course, A-levels	JAD
Probation Officer	4	5 including English, Maths	Social Sciences, Statistics	A-levels, Diploma in Social Work	KEB
Psychologist/ Psychotherapist	4	5 including English, Maths	Science, Social Sciences, Statistics	A-levels, degree	KEL
Religious Ministry (Priest, Minister etc)	1/2/3/4		English, Religious Studies, History	A-levels, degree, Theological training	FAM
Residential Care Assistant (eg Homes for the Elderly)	Entry/1/2/3		English, Home Economics, Social Sciences	College course in a Care subject or pre-social work	KEB
Social Worker	4	5 including English, Maths	Statistics, Social Sciences	A-levels, Diploma in Social Work	KEB

Useful websites

Charities/Voluntary Organisation Work – www.ncvo-vol.org.uk
Psychologist/Psychotherapist– www.bps.org.uk
Social Worker – www.ccetsw.org.uk

I'm Thinking About a Career . . . in Transport or Travel

Job title	Minimum entry level	Essential GCSEs	Useful subjects	Other academic/training requirements	CLCI reference
Air Cabin Crew	2/3	Modern Languages, English, Maths	Geography, Home Economics/ Food Studies	A-levels, experience in nursing, care work, catering	YAB
Driver (Bus, Taxi, Lorry etc)	Entry/1		Motor Vehicle Studies	Car driving licence pre-entry	YAD
Merchant Navy Deck Officer	3/4	4 including Maths, Science, English	Nautical Studies, Design/Technology, Geography	Maths/Science A-levels, degree	YAL
Merchant Navy Deck/ Catering Rating	1	3 including Maths, Science, English	Nautical Studies, Home Economics/ Food Studies		YAL
Merchant Navy Engineering Officer	2/3/4	4 including Maths, Science, English	Nautical Studies, Design/Technology	Maths/Physics A-levels, degree	YAL
Railway Fitter/Electrician	1/2	English, Maths, Science	Design/Technology, Engineering		YAF

Road Transport Manager	3/4	5 including English, Maths	Economics, Business Studies, ICT	A-levels, degree	YAD
Travel Agency Work	2/3/4	4 including English, Maths	Modern Languages, Geography, Business Studies, ICT	A-levels, degree, Diploma course with Travel option	GAX
Travel Courier/ Resort Representative	1/2/3	Modern Languages	English, Maths, Geography	A-levels	GAX

Useful websites

Railway Industry – www.ritc.org.uk
Road Transport Manager/Logistics and Transport – www.iolt.org.uk
Travel and Tourism – www.careercompass.co.uk

10. HOW HAS GCSE WORKED IN PRACTICE?

How do GCSE results compare with the old system?

Generally, very favourably. The overall pattern is one of higher standards, although reservations about some aspects of the examination and its assessment procedures have led to some of the changes described in this book.

The year 2000 saw the highest proportion of A* to C grades awarded for GCSE, with 56.6% achieving at least one grade A* to C in full GCSE courses; 61.1% of girls achieved a C or above, compared to 51.9% of boys.

In 1999 88.5% of 15-year-olds gained at least five GCSEs at grades A*–G; 95% of 15-year-olds were entered for one or more GCSEs or GNVQ equivalent, and 90% for five or more.

The government uses GCSE achievement as its principal way of measuring improvement in teaching and learning for 15–16 year olds. Its National Targets for the year 2002 include the aim of having half of the nation's 16-year-olds getting five A*–C GCSE passes and 95% getting at least one.

There is special concern about low achievement in English and Maths. Only 40% of 16-year-olds scored at least a C in both English and Maths in 1999 (43% of girls, 36% of boys). 87% scored at least a G in both subjects.

How will I get my results?

Each awarding body is responsible for publishing the results of its examinations on a jointly agreed date, usually towards the end of August.

The results will be sent to your school or college, which will then forward them to you. Some schools and colleges make arrangements for candidates to collect their results in person (often later on the day of their arrival). Your school or college will always tell you the date you can expect to receive or collect them.

How can I be sure that my grade will be accurate?

Proven inaccuracies have been very few in number, measured against the millions of subject entries. Remember that the system of checking marking and results includes impartial observers and that the checking system is *very* thorough.

There are six levels of enquiry service provided by the awarding bodies, ranging from a quick clerical check to a full re-mark and report. Barely half a per cent of all GCSE candidates make an enquiry, either individually or through their schools.

If you do wish to use the appeals system to query your GCSE grade, in the first instance you should appeal to your school or college. If they think a mistake has been made they will put in an appeal to the awarding body on your behalf; it costs about £15 for an exam script to be re-examined, but schools are reimbursed if they win their case. The school has to submit any such results enquiry to the relevant awarding body within about four weeks of the results being published. An Examinations Appeals Board (EAB) was set up in 1999. Its role is to help ensure that candidates, parents, schools and colleges are satisfied that the grades awarded are fair and as accurate as possible. The EAB only becomes involved when the awarding bodies' own procedures have been exhausted.

In Northern Ireland the CCEA is unique in offering an accelerated service that re-marks papers within two weeks for an extra fee.

In Scotland anyone can query results, though not everyone can instigate the formal appeal. The Scottish system suffered a considerable reverse in summer 2000, when flaws in a new SQA computer system meant that 4000 candidates received incomplete or inaccurate Standard grade results.

But, before even considering the appeals process, remember that your teachers are in a good position to make an accurate assessment of your work. The likelihood of an error in the marking is very low.

The DfEE is actively encouraging more openness in the examining body procedures. It wants to see greater freedom of information, improved accountability and clearer feedback to schools. From 2000, candidates in English, Irish, Welsh and Mathematics will be able to request access to their own scripts. Requests are to be made through the school (with private candidates able to arrange access direct through the relevant awarding body). This scheme may be extended across other subjects from 2001.

Schools also have an independent right to request scripts, in order to support staff in their teaching, but candidates have the right to prevent their schools requesting their scripts by writing to the headteacher.

Schools can also request photocopies of re-marked scripts, along with the outcome of enquiries on results for GCSE scripts involved in the access scheme (covering English, Irish, Welsh and Mathematics).

The awarding bodies also provide revision guidance through broadcasters and the media, along with past papers, student guides and exam resources on the Web. They support teachers through a range of materials, including teachers' guides, coursework guides, examiner reports, videos, tapes and classroom delivery materials.

The awarding bodies also provide a vast annual in-service education and training programme covering current and new specifications – with opportunities for teachers to participate in trial marking and to ask questions of senior examiners and specification developers.

Has GCSE really proved suitable for everyone?

GCSE is open to anyone at school or college, whatever their ability. However, it is not always the right course or qualification for some less able students. This is because of the high requirement for literacy and the demands of coursework.

It is difficult to provide courses and exams that will suit the whole age group. An increasing number of courses are being provided for students who are unlikely to achieve a GCSE grade G or an equivalent qualification (Foundation GNVQ or NVQ level 1). There are Entry Level Certificates in:

- the subjects that students will have studied up to the age of 14; and also
- in broader vocational areas that are more like the GNVQ subjects.

Students can achieve Entry Level Certificates at three different levels, broadly equivalent to National Curriculum levels 1–3. Students can take Entry Level Certificates alongside GCSEs, GNVQs, Vocational GCSEs or NVQs. They are assessed in tasks that may be written, spoken or practical.

Most of these courses have been developed by the main awarding bodies, with a few local syllabuses also approved by the QCA and ACCAC. Subject areas available include:

- Art
- Business Studies
- Catering
- Childcare/Childcare & Development
- Design & Technology
- English
- Food Studies
- French
- Geography
- Graphical & Material Studies
- Hairdressing
- History
- Humanities
- Information Technology
- Land Studies
- Leisure & Tourism
- Life Skills

- Manufacturing
- Materials Technology
- Mathematics
- Media Studies
- Modern Foreign Languages
- Modern Foreign Language Skills for Work
- Motor Vehicle & Road User Studies
- Music
- Office Practice
- Physical Education
- Religious Education/Studies
- Retail
- Science
- Textiles
- Travel & Tourism
- Welsh
- Welsh Second Language.

Your school will be able to tell you whether it is operating any of these alternatives.

QCA, ACCAC and CCEA have now approved 80 different awards, and more are on stream. Entry level awards are available in vocational areas such as retail, leisure and tourism, and manufacturing. Entry level awards in basic skills, such as literacy and numeracy, are also being developed and will soon be ready for accreditation.

Is it true that girls do better than boys?

In 1999, 88.5% of 15-year-olds gained at least five GCSEs at grades A*–G: 90.6% of girls and 88.9% of boys; 89% of students overall attempted a GCSE in English, Maths and Science, and 36% achieved grades A*–C in all three subjects. In this respect, 39% of the girls were successful, compared with 33% of the boys.

When foreign languages are included, 34% of girls achieved grades A*–C, compared with 24% of boys. Boys did slightly better in Geography – 23%, compared with girls' 21%.

What advice can you give me on which level of exam to choose?

In subjects where there is a choice of level you must first of all listen to the advice of your subject teachers. Try to avoid the temptation of ignoring what they say just because the alternative option holds out the possibility of a higher – or safer – grade. They are probably the best judges of your potential.

What difference has GCSE made to the way my subjects are taught?

Most importantly, it has raised standards of teaching. Her Majesty's Inspectorate (HMI) visits to schools have indicated a significant improvement in the standard of lessons observed.

In particular, the HMIs found that study for the new exam has raised both students' motivation and performance, and teaching quality. They stated that 'teachers appear to have become more aware of what [students] are capable of achieving'.

GCSE has led to a marked improvement in oral and written work, and more and better practical and investigative work. It has increased the ability of students to show what they know, understand and can do, especially in their coursework. The additional emphasis given to positive achievement in both coursework and the exams is probably the greatest success of GCSE.

Will GCSE prepare me for study at higher level?

HMIs expressed the view that it is 'sufficient of a challenge to form a sound intellectual basis for students going on to A-level'. GCSE has had a positive impact on the numbers of young people staying on in full-time education in order to take A-levels or equivalent courses.

A-levels themselves have begun to change and are likely to be revised further, partly to reflect the differences in the GCSE syllabuses. In a more positive sense they should also change in order to take maximum benefit from the new skills being measured by the GCSE.

Remember that you need to do *really well* in a subject at GCSE to consider taking it at A-level. Even a C grade is not a good indicator for A-level success in some subjects. This does *not* mean that you can't take A-levels (or other higher-level courses) of which you have no previous experience, as long as this is not simply an 'escape route' and you do have some evidence of your ability to cope.

11. THE GCSE IN NORTHERN IRELAND

In Northern Ireland the Northern Ireland Council for the Curriculum, Examinations and Assessment (CCEA) advises the government on curriculum, assessment and examination matters. The CCEA is responsible for conducting key stage assessments and the conduct of GCSE and GCE examinations.

The CCEA also regulates standards in GCSE, GCE and GNVQ examinations in Northern Ireland. GCSE syllabuses and examinations in Northern Ireland comply with the GCSE general and subject criteria, taking into account where necessary the distinctive features of the Northern Ireland common curriculum.

The CCEA is conducting a review of the Northern Ireland curriculum. The framework of what should be taught in schools will be agreed following a period of initial consultation. Then, from April–June 2001, the CCEA will send proposals for each Key Stage to schools for further consultation. Final proposals will be sent to the Department of Education (DENI) in November 2001. Northern Ireland schools will then begin delivering the revised curriculum – including new GCSE courses – in September 2002.

What GCSE subjects are available in Northern Ireland?

- Additional Mathematics
- Art & Design
- Business Studies
- Drama
- Economics
- English
- English Literature
- French
- Geography
- German
- History
- Home Economics
- Home Economics: Child Development
- Information & Communications Technology (ICT) – short course
- Information Systems
- Irish

- Irish (Gaeilge)
- Latin
- Mathematics
- Motor Vehicle & Road User Studies
- Music
- Physical Education
- Religious Studies
- Religious Studies – short course
- Science: Biology
- Science: Chemistry
- Science: double award
- Science: Physics
- Science: single award
- Social & Environmental Studies
- Spanish
- Technology & Design.

In Northern Ireland the Key Stage 4 (Years 11 and 12) curriculum consists of six Areas of Study, six educational (cross-curricular) themes and a course of religious education.

What are these areas of study?

The six Areas of Study are:

- English
- Mathematics
- Science & Technology
- The Environment and Society
- Creative & Expressive Studies (Physical Education)
- Language Studies.

Students who have taken GCSE in either English or Mathematics at the end of Year 11 do not have to follow the Key Stage 4 programme of study. However, they must take another 'cognate' subject, eg English Literature (in the case of English) or Additional Mathematics or Statistics (in the case of Mathematics).

National Curriculum programmes of study define the essential content of each subject and are the basis for planning, teaching, learning and assessment objectives. They operate in most Areas of Study. All courses in compulsory subjects that do not have programmes of study now have to be approved by DENI on the advice of CCEA.

In The Environment and Society there is now a choice between:

(a) a course from History/Geography/Business Studies/Home Economics; or
(b) an approved course in Economics/Politics or modular provision selected from a range of modules to include Law in our Lives, Environmental Education, Information Technology, Health/Sex Education, Economic Awareness, Cultural Heritage, Careers Education.

Language Studies provision now consists of an approved course, eg GCSE or GNVQ unit(s) or Graded Objective in Modern Languages (GOML).

Will I have much choice?

Reduction in the statutory curriculum time is intended to allow schools further flexibility to meet students' needs. For example, this can be used to provide additional time for the compulsory subjects, to offer additional courses from within the Area of Study framework, or to provide additional elements such as Personal and Social Education and Careers Guidance.

What about coursework?

Coursework weightings are also different in Northern Ireland. The maximum allocations for coursework are as follows:

Art & Design	60%
Biology: Human	24%
Business Studies	20%
CDT Design & Communication	45%
CDT Design & Realisation	50%
Classical Civilisation	20%
Economics	20%
English	40%
English Literature	30%
Geography	20%
History	30%
Mathematics	20%
Religious Studies	30%
Science: Biology	24%
Science: Chemistry	24%
Science: double award	28%
Science: Physics	24%
Science: single award	25%
Social Science	30%
Technology	45%

Do we all sit the same exams?

No. There are again tiering arrangements, but these are different in Northern Ireland. The tiers of entry for Northern Ireland National Curriculum subjects are:

Mathematics	Tier P	grades D–G
	Tier Q	A*–D
Science	Tier P	D–G
(Double/Single award)	Tier Q	B–D (B–E for single award)
	Tier R	A*–B
English	Tier S	C–G
	Tier T	A*–D

Important addresses in Northern Ireland

Department of Education Northern Ireland
New St Andrew's House
Balloo Road
Bangor
County Down
BT19 2PR
02891 279279
www.deni.gov.uk

Northern Ireland Council for the Curriculum, Examinations and Assessment
29 Clarendon Road
Clarendon Dock
Belfast
BT1 3BG
028 9026 1200
www.ccea.org.uk

12. ... AND IN SCOTLAND

Is the structure of the secondary curriculum and examinations the same as in the rest of the UK?

No. There are several major differences in the Scottish system. Firstly, students in Scotland begin their secondary schooling when they are about 12 years of age. The curriculum is divided into three stages, the first two of which are compulsory. In the first two years of secondary school (S1 and S2), students follow a broad and balanced educational programme. Towards the end of S2 they choose the courses they will study in S3 and S4.

Does this mean that there is more choice for 14- and 15-year-olds in Scotland?

Not entirely. In effect, Scotland has a national curriculum for this age group, since all schools are expected to follow certain guiding principles, as defined by the Scottish Qualifications Authority (SQA).

All students have to continue studying English, Mathematics, a modern European language and a Science course at S3 and S4. In addition, schools are asked to ensure that students select additional full or short courses meeting the requirements of eight 'modes' or areas of study:

Language and Communication
Mathematical Studies and Applications
Scientific Studies and Applications
Social and Environmental Studies
Technological Activities and Applications
Creative and Aesthetic Activities
Physical Education
Religious and Moral Education

What sort of school-leaving examinations are there?

At the end of S4 the majority of students take examinations leading to the Scottish Certificate of Education (SCE). The courses taken lead to awards at Standard (S) Grade and to short course awards, recorded on the Scottish Certificate of Education.

Do I have to take exams in all the different modes?

Not as such. The S3 and S4 courses are meant to give each student adequate experience in all the modes, but the S Grade courses are not an exact match to the individual modes. A single course may contribute to several different modes.

Students may cover the entire mode requirement by choosing a Core course. For example, it is possible to meet the Technological Activities and Applications requirement by taking an S Grade course in Computing Studies, Craft & Design, Home Economics, Office & Information Studies *or* Technological Studies *or* relevant short courses *or* appropriate activities from these courses. It is also possible to meet this same mode requirement by taking other courses from a range of elective options.

Are all these options available in all the schools?

No. Larger schools are normally able to offer a wider choice than smaller schools. National syllabuses also allow schools some flexibility in deciding on course content and on teaching and learning methods. So there may be differences in the teaching of a particular course between one school and another.

How much time will I have to study each subject?

There are recommended minimum and maximum time allocations for each student, based on the assumption that the syllabuses for English and Mathematics would need five 40-minute periods a week and those for other full courses four periods. The normal minimum time requirement (in hours) for each of the modes, over the two-year period, is as follows:

Language and Communication	360
Mathematical Studies and Applications	200
Scientific Studies and Applications	160
Social and Environmental Studies	160
Technological Activities and Applications	80
Creative and Aesthetic Activities	80
Physical Education	80
Religious and Moral Education	80

The total of 1200 hours allocated to this core of the eight modes represents approximately 70% of the time available to students throughout S3 and S4.

What happens for the rest of the time?

In the remaining 30% of available class time schools are able to offer a variety of short or modular courses of varying lengths. The most common format for such courses is that of modules leading to the award of the National Certificate by SQA. The SQA modules include a number of courses that serve to complement the curriculum at S3 and S4.

The SQA also provides a limited range of short courses that are certificated on the SCE. These are intended to provide candidates with an extension or enrichment of their curriculum in and after the third year of secondary education. The short courses offered in this way are:

- Classical Studies
- Creative & Aesthetic Studies
- Electronics
- European Studies
- Geology
- Graphic Communication
- Health Studies
- Nautical Studies
- Religious & Moral Education
- Statistics
- Technological Studies.

These short courses leading to certificated awards are 40-hour units that are internally assessed and externally moderated. Awards are ungraded and are recorded on the same certificate as Standard (or Higher (H)) Grade awards.

Schools can also offer short courses of their own design, which do not lead to national certification.

Are Standard Grade courses and exams the same for all?

Not in all cases. In some areas, such as Mathematics, students follow courses at three levels, ie to suit different levels of ability. In other areas, such as English, the course is the same for all, but the skills to be acquired are differentiated to suit the different ability groups.

What is the grading system for the Standard Grade exams?

Standard Grade awards are made in terms of a seven-point numerical scale 1–7, where 1 is the highest award. The attainment levels for grades 1–6 are specified by the Grade Related Criteria (GRC), which are available from the SQA on request. Grade 7 indicates that the course was completed but without evidence of significant attainment.

For most courses there are three separate examination papers at the end of the two years. They are set for Credit, General and Foundation levels.

Credit papers lead to awards at grade 1 or 2, General papers to awards at grade 3 or 4 and Foundation papers to awards at grade 5 or 6.

Normally students take examinations covering two pairs of grades, either grades 1–4 or grades 3–6. This is intended to ensure that all students have the best opportunity to gain an award that reflects their real ability and achievement.

A Standard Grade award of grade 3 or better is equivalent to a GCSE award at grade C or better.

What else do I need to know about the assessment system?

It is essentially a performance- or criteria-related method of assessment. In other words, the award is based on the achievements of the individual student, measured against stated standards, rather than on how that individual's achievement compares with that of other candidates.

In order to achieve a particular grade within a particular level candidates have to give evidence of achievement in all the basic aspects of the subject. For example, in English, candidates will receive separate assessments for Reading, Writing and Talking as well as an overall grade. A Profile of Performance stating all grades then appears on the Certificate beside the overall award for the course. To continue the example of English, an individual student's award might therefore be reported in this way:

Subject	Overall Award	Profile of Performance	
English	3	Reading	3
		Writing	2
		Talking	4

How will this be assessed?

In a variety of different ways. In most courses candidates will have to demonstrate attainment in oral or practical skills, and these skills will usually be assessed internally by the class teacher on the basis of work done during the course.

Other aspects, such as Writing in English, will be assessed on the basis of a folio submitted to the SQA, together with a written examination. Yet others will be assessed through a written examination alone.

In all cases, even where a part of the course is assessed externally, teachers will have submitted estimated grades to the SQA. These can be used to improve the SQA grades in the case of any disagreement.

If an assessment is not available for any part of the course, for whatever reason, no overall grade can be given for the course. The only exception to this is when a candidate is not able to do part of the course because of a particular handicap or impairment.

What about the assessment of short courses?

The individual school is responsible for assessing candidates taking short courses, with the SQA moderating school assessments to ensure national standards.

The SCE then records any SQA short courses that have been completed successfully.

What happens at 16+?

There is a further, optional stage of one or two years for students aged 16 to 18 who wish to stay on at school. At present, over 75% of S4 students are returning to school for S5.

Students who achieve a Credit level award at Standard Grade will normally progress to take Highers or SVQ3. Students who achieve General normally go on to an Intermediate 2 or SVQ1 or SVQ2.

A Foundation pass in Standard Grade can lead to Intermediate 1, although some students may do best to broaden their experience at Access 3 first.

A student who does not manage Standard Grade can attempt Access 2 or 3 units as early as Third Year and progress to additional units at these levels after that, or attempt a Skillstart award.

Higher Still

A new system of post-16 qualifications was introduced in Scotland in 1999, administered by the Scottish Qualifications Authority. The aim of the 'Higher Still' Programme is to bring together all existing awards into a single, coherent post-16 system. The new qualifications include National Units, National Courses and Scottish Group Awards (SGAs) and cater for anyone studying after Standard Grade, whether in school or further education college. They are meant to sit alongside and link to Scottish Vocational Qualifications (SVQs).

The new system is based on units, each a qualification in its own right. So, students who pass the units, but not the external examination, still get a national qualification. The units, normally of 40 or 80 hours teaching time, cover both academic and vocational subjects. Units may be taken on a free-standing basis or grouped together into courses.

Units and courses are structured into a series of levels: Access 1, Access 2, Access 3, Intermediate 1 and 2, Higher and Advanced Higher (the last replaces the CSYS).

How Standard Grades relate to Higher Still and SVQs

Standard Grade		Higher Still		SVQs
		Advanced Higher		
		Higher	=	SVQ 3
Credit	=	Intermediate 2	=	SVQ 2
General	=	Intermediate 1	=	SVQ 1
Foundation	=	Access		

Important addresses in Scotland

Scottish Office Education and Industry Department
Rathgael House
St James Centre
Edinburgh
EH1 3SY
0131 556 8400
www.scotland.gov.uk

13. LIFE AFTER GCSE – OPTIONS AT 16

My options at 16 – how will they affect my choice of GCSEs?

In another two years you will be facing another decision – one that will shape your future. And the choice will be even greater, but you are laying the foundation of that choice now, by the options you are making in your selection of GCSE subjects.

So, before you make your final selection of GCSEs, think carefully about what you might decide to do later on.

The options at 16 are very wide indeed, but these are the major ones.

Getting a job

There's no denying that for some school is just a chore – they can't wait to get out and earn their own living. However, relatively few employers are recruiting at 16. Of those that are, you should certainly be looking more seriously at those offering further training, preferably leading to a National Vocational Qualification. You need to think about what GCSEs would be preferred, or required, to start a job at 16.

Getting a job with NVQ training

You can work with a company or organisation that offers training leading to an NVQ. You would usually attend a college or training centre one day a week, to pick up extra skills that will back up those you are learning in the workplace. This work-based qualification will be related to the skill requirements of the specific job. You will not need any particular qualifications to go on to NVQ Level 1 training. NVQ Level 2 requires GCSEs at grades D–G, while NVQ Level 3 requires 4 GCSEs at grade C or above.

Modern Apprenticeships

Modern Apprenticeships have been available since September 1994. They are geared to individual needs and have been very successful in providing high quality training for young people. Foundation Modern Apprenticeships provide training to at least NVQ Level 2, but with the addition of Key Skills. Advanced Modern Apprenticeships are for young people training to get at least an NVQ Level 3 (equivalent to two A-levels), plus Key Skills. An Advanced Modern Apprenticeship lasts about three years and can lead to further progression and higher qualifications.

Training with a training provider

If jobs with Modern Apprenticeships or NVQ training are not immediately available, a good alternative is to apply for a training place with a local training provider. There will probably be a range of training provider organisations in your area and you can seek information and advice on them from your careers or personal adviser. Training providers offer different training opportunities, leading to NVQs and/or Modern Apprenticeships. Whereas you get wages if training as an employee, as a trainee you get a training allowance (and sometimes help with travelling costs).

College courses

Your local college of further education (or tertiary college) is likely to be offering a range of full- and part-time courses. Full-time vocational courses on offer may include GNVQs and vocational A-levels, and BTEC/Edexcel First Diploma and National Diploma courses.

The same college may also be offering other courses in competition with, or possibly complementing, the local school sixth form(s), in A/AS levels and GCSEs.

Staying on at school

This will often involve taking AS and A-levels – and now this includes the new vocational A-levels (replacing Advanced GNVQs). Courses at this level are essential if you want to go on to take a degree.

Post-16, the vocational areas available at Advanced Level (and the other two GNVQ Levels) include:

• Art and Design
• Business
• Construction and the Built Environment
• Engineering
• Health and Social Care
• Hospitality and Catering
• Information Technology
• Land and Environment
• Leisure and Recreation

- Manufacturing
- Media: Communication and Production
- Performing Arts
- Retail and Distributive Services
- Science
- Travel and Tourism.

If taking A-levels, you'll probably be expected to take four or five subjects over the two-year period, including the new AS level. This new AS qualification is equivalent to the first year of the full A-level and is worth 50% of the marks.

The full A-level qualification will normally be made up of six modules. The first three modules form the AS level for the subject.

The vocational A-levels have a similar structure. There is a three-unit vocational AS in Business, Engineering, Health & Social Care, and Information Technology. A six-unit vocational course is a full A-level. This standardisation of structure makes it much easier to mix and match vocational and other A/AS levels.

The subjects you have taken at GCSE are bound to influence your choice of A/AS levels. A/AS levels are of a high standard and in some subjects it may not be easy to cope with the A/AS level syllabus unless you have studied the subject on a GCSE course – Languages and Sciences are examples of this. So, ask yourself which A/AS levels you might want to do before choosing your GCSEs.

Some of the subjects offered at A/AS level include the learning of specific practical skills. In some schools and colleges you can study Dance, Art or Sports Studies at A/AS level.

Other options in the sixth form or at college

Many schools and colleges offer Foundation or Intermediate Level GNVQ courses for students in Year 12 onwards.

For GNVQ Intermediate courses students are normally expected to have achieved something like four GCSEs at grades D–G or a Foundation GNVQ (or an NVQ at Level 1).

Entry on to GNVQ Foundation Level courses does not require any formal qualifications, although applicants need to show the ability to benefit from the course.

You may find that you are also able to take GCSEs in the sixth form. These are usually two-year courses, but sometimes there is the option of special one-year courses, especially in new subject areas. Coursework will still normally be a feature of these courses, but the syllabus will be designed to ensure you can carry it out within one year.

14. MAKING THE CHOICE

The National Curriculum has already greatly limited the number of options open to students in Years 10 and 11 (Years 11 and 12 in Northern Ireland). However, if your school continues to operate a system with any element of choice in the subjects to be taken at GCSE, it is important that you should think carefully about your choice. This book should have helped you get all the facts you need. You should now be ready to make your final choice.

Use this checklist to make your selection.

- Make a list of all the subjects your school is offering.
- Tick subjects that are essential for your career.
- Tick all the subjects your school insists that you take.
- Tick any subjects you enjoy/are good at/want to take.
- Tick any of the new subjects being offered that you would like to try or think would be useful.
- Check to see if you have at least one subject from each of the major subject groups, ie:
    English
    Maths
    Modern Foreign Languages
    Sciences
    Humanities
    Creative Subjects (including Technology)
    and make sure you have taken advice before leaving out any one group.
- Count up the number of subjects you have ticked. If it comes to more than six, check with your teachers how many subjects they think you can cope with.
- Check the coursework commitment in each subject with your teachers.
- If there are too many subjects or the coursework commitment is too high, work through this list again, being more selective.
- Remember that there are other people as well as your subject teachers who you can talk to – your careers (or personal) adviser, careers teacher, form tutor, year tutor and, of course, your family.

Now, how does it look?

Horrendous?
Horrifying?
Difficult?
Look through the checklist again and be even more selective.

Or:

Hard work?
Interesting?
OK?
Just right?
GO FOR IT!

But what if I do choose the wrong subjects, what can I do?

Don't panic! It happens all the time.

It could be that you will suddenly get a new career idea and will realise you need to be studying something else. If you have chosen wisely in the first place it is unlikely that many of the subjects you have opted for will be wrong. So, if you are partway through your GCSEs, the answer is to keep on studying and get the best possible grades you can in the subjects you are taking. That will always stand you in good stead. Who knows, you might change your mind yet again.

Then, when you get to the sixth form or move on to a college, you can take the extra subjects you need. Because you will be that much older, you should be able to take them in one year instead of the normal two – that is one of the advantages of the GCSE system.

My GCSE decisions

Subject groups

English	Maths	Sciences	Humanities	Creative subjects	Modern languages

1 ——————————————————————————————

2 ——————————————————————————————

3 ——————————————————————————————

OTHER SOURCES OF REFERENCE

Your school's *Options* booklet.

Which Way Now (COIC). This booklet considers the implications of subject choices for later career decisions and routes. It is also available on the World Wide Web (www.dfee.gov.uk/wwn/)

It's Your Choice (COIC) is also written for students and is about the choices to be made at 16+.

You can obtain both these free publications by phoning 08000 96 66 26.

Subjects and Exams for 14- to 16-year-olds (QCA) (available also in Bengali, Chinese, Greek, Gujarati, Hindi, Punjabi, Turkish, Urdu, Vietnamese and in Braille and on cassette). Phone 020 8561 4499.

GCSE Regulations and Criteria (QCA/ACCAC).

If you want a different angle on HE

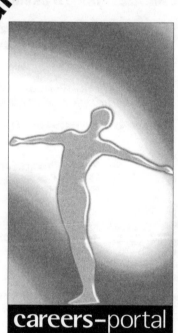

www.careers-portal.co.uk

careers-portal

The site that will give you the truth... however bad!